No Food for You Missy

Make Food Your Friend
You Are Not Alone

By Annette Son

No Food for You Missy
Make Food Your Friend
You Are Not Alone

©2019 by Annette Son

Disclaimer: This is my very personal experience, my own opinions about certain foods and other things, and the fact that I just don't like Brussels sprouts is not meant to offend anybody.

Please take this as a personal discovery and ranting session, nothing more.

The people I mention are all real and dear to me (although I changed the names), and I love you all for encouraging me and staying with me through this endeavor!

ISBN: 9781672803120

Dedication

For my husband and my boys, I love you so very much!

~Annette Son

Introduction

Hi! My name is Annette ☺

I am an author, life coach, private tutor, and most of all, a Mom. I live in Southern California with one husband, two sons and three birds, all of them helping me not to feel bored throughout the day!

I've lived a fairly normal life until one day my happy Nutella-toast-in-the-morning-days came to a very abrupt halt and were, involuntarily, replaced by… I can't even describe it… well, you'll have to read and see what it is that I now have for breakfast and other meals, as well as the snacks I've suffered through…

The reason for this change was a truly accidental discovery of allergies and food sensitivities. Researchers estimate that about 32 million Americans suffer from food allergies. And yet, less than 4% of adults have this condition documented by their doctors. On the other hand, there are about 170 food ingredients that can trigger allergies. People can experience symptons and not even know that these are caused by the food they eat.

This was an area I knew almost nothing about when my personal discovery hit.

As a result, not by personal choice but rather as directed by my naturopath, I found myself thrown into the very unfamiliar territory of a world that is gluten-free, free of dairy, yeast, eggs, poultry, nuts and seeds, etc., etc., as well as, mostly free of ideas for dinner.

I've learned a lot and thought I would share this knowledge with you, along with my experiences, good and bad, and for sure the funny ones!

This is my one-year experience on a very specific elimination diet!

So, I invite you to read my diary of what happened when I changed my nutrition COMPLETELY, turning my life upside down..., and if you are having similar issues, just know that YOU ARE NOT ALONE!

Diary

Day 1 – *Feeling of the Day*: Floored!

Soooooooooooo, I've just been diagnosed with multiple food allergies and sensitivities, and I did not expect this at all! My doctor was doing a few check-ups for various things (I don't even need to go into them here) and as a measure of being extra careful, asked if I would agree to have a comprehensive food allergy panel done.

"Sure," I agreed, not expecting much. After all, I am a pretty healthy person, everyone around me thinks that I am healthy, and I have never had any reactions to food, other than a prickly tongue when I ate a persimmon. But how often does one eat persimmons? Maybe that one was going bad, so I didn't pay much attention to it.

But in any case, here is the verdict:

No more wheat, gluten, yeast, bran, quinoa or amaranth grains, eggs, milk or other dairy products, no nuts or seeds of any kind, chicken or other birds, lamb, coconut, banana, pineapple, spinach (!!), salmon and some other fish, and green tea!

Who in the world is sensitive to green tea?!?!? WHAT?????

At this point, the safest food choice left is ketchup!

Yup, that and fries because I can have potatoes!

I almost fell off my chair, because the above list is pretty much 100% my diet. And that, in retrospect, is probably the reason why I've developed sensitivities or allergies to these various foods. So, despite eating what looked like a super healthy diet all these years, I've been damaging my gut, and the antidote apparently is In-N-Out Burgers – protein style!!

The Doctor said, "No birds."

I asked him: "Do I get to keep my pet parakeets?"

He replied, "Yes, just don't eat them!"

Well, I must do this gut healing diet, staying away from the listed foods above for one year minimum. Let's just say one year... I need help!

I'm not a cook, and therefore already struggle to feed my family of four. I have two sons in middle school who should be eating better than they are. I am trying! Really, I am! But it's not easy when cooking does not come naturally. It doesn't flow for me.

My husband, Rob, cooks well so he provides many of the dinners, but I had already made a commitment to do better at providing healthy and well-balanced dinners for the family starting this year.

And they've all been brave at trying the foods!

But this new development has just added a whole new dimension!

Day 2 – *Feeling of the Day*: Despairing

Yesterday's news was funny, I thought. Today's visit at the health food store was not.

I went in to get some advice and find products that would fit the criteria of my specific food limitations. It took a lot of label reading to see if any of the evil foods were included in the various cereals, alternative milk choices, bread spreads and most importantly, bread!

The very nice salesperson tried to find me bread. I am German; I must have bread in the house! But it must be gluten-free and without eggs, dairy or yeast – the choices are extremely slim. We looked at several loaves, reading the ingredients carefully, but there was always one ingredient that wasn't allowed for me. If it contained no gluten, then it might have had dairy or eggs. If none of that, there were seeds in it. It was getting a bit frustrating!

He finally said, "Wait, I think I have one type of bread that will be okay!"

Excitedly, we walked over to another cooler that contained more specialty breads. He looked around the shelf, read the labels, and finally stuck his hand deep down into a hole that had formed around the other loaves. After a quick moment, he straightened up and said, "I'm all out of that one."

I had a sinking feeling that this year was not going to be so funny after all.

An hour and a half and $135 later, I walked out of the store, drove home and picked up my good friend Kate to run an errand with her. She had read my text message from earlier that I could use some company today, and when she approached the car, she looked at me, expecting really bad news.

I told her it wasn't life or death-type news, rather a severe quality of life-crisis for this chocolate, bread and cheese-loving German. Since Kate is a good cook, I wanted to pick her brain for some ideas.

Specifically, where to find protein! After our errand, Kate came into our house with me, looked at my forbidden foods list, and suggested a curry bean dish that she makes. Then I gave her a couple of bags of food that I had sorted out because all of it was no longer allowed in my pantry.

The revelation hit: I should either move to Japan right away (the Japanese cuisine is naturally gluten-free) or exist on rice and beans for a year.

Day 5 – *Feeling of the Day*: Lost

Where can I find protein??

The doctor had given me a list of complementary proteins, mainly from plant sources, which would form complete proteins the way the body needs them. The list was divided into three categories: Grains & Legumes, Nuts/Seeds & Legumes, and Grains & Dairy Foods.

I immediately crossed out the entire section of nuts/seeds & legumes as well as the grains & dairy foods. This left me with grains & legumes.

This category listed fourteen suggested food combinations of various grains combined in a dish with a legume type. I crossed out all those that contained wheat and the other forbidden grains. I now have rice and beans left.

I was never that much into food. Preparation had to be quick and easy, although not fast food. I did try to eat healthy for sure. 'Foodie' means to me that I eat whatever I feel like, nothing extravagant by any means. I hate the word 'delish', and I have no clue what tempeh is or what it even looks like. However, when nearly all your favorite and comforting choices of food are taken away in one drastic swipe, then suddenly food becomes a lot more important!

I really do feel for all those people that have much more severe reactions to food than I do. This is really starting not to be fun!

Day 7 – *Feeling of the Day*: Sliver of hope

Hey, I found two breakfast foods so far, things are looking up!

There's a type of bread that is strictly made from brown rice flour. I found it in the freezer section at a big health food store. I have to toast it twice to mask the heavy and dry texture, but then I can top it with peanut butter and jelly and there's my protein for breakfast. This one is actually tasty! ☺

For variation, I started looking for cereal. Now this presented a real quest-like action in the cereal aisle. Gluten-free, but no nuts or seeds either. I found one: Cornflakes!!

Now, I need to find alternative milk, but none of those almond or cashew milks (because of the nuts). I started with soy milk, but not good in the long run (too much soy is no good either), but at least, I've got something to eat in the mornings now.

I am also experimenting with alternative creamers for my afternoon coffee. I started with soy, but I feel like I have tofu in my coffee. Just not cool!

There's also vanilla soy creamer as well as vanilla coconut creamer (apparently, I can have coconut about twice a week). Everything in the alternative milk department is either scary or vanilla. I'm going to be super vanilla allergic by the end of this!

Day 9 – *Feeling of the Day*: Ashamed

I had a horrible experience today! Hubby suggested we go out for lunch to one of our favorite Greek food places nearby. Of course, that was not the horrible part. In fact, since I've been struggling to find foods and making things work, I was grateful for the opportunity to just go and have somebody else deal with feeding me!

We got to the restaurant and I ordered a Greek salad with Gyro meat on top (need protein) and thought I was so clever when I placed my order as I told the very nice man that I did not want the pita bread or tzatziki dip! I was so pleased with myself and proud that I could be going to a restaurant, well aware of no gluten or dairy!

Well, our meals arrived and mine was topped with lots and lots of feta cheese.

Rob and I looked at each other and the deepest "Oh no..........!" escaped me. I'd forgotten to tell the waiter no cheese!

The waiter realized there was a problem and asked what was wrong. I was ready to just order another salad and pay for it, when all that came out of my mouth was "I can't have cheese!"

"Oh," said the waiter. He swiftly took my plate and walked back to the kitchen area. I watched and thought he would just have the cook try to pick the cheese out of the salad, but after a short moment of hesitation, he dumped THE WHOLE SALAD into the trash!

I was truly horrified because I had caused such a waste! I felt terrible.

A moment later, he brought another salad without cheese and I apologized for my neglect, but of course, he didn't want to hear about it, being all kind and of service and all.

After we finished eating, I walked up to the cashier and tried to pay for the second salad, but they insisted it was not necessary.

I still feel really bad!!

Day 12 – *Feeling of the Day*: Hmmmm? Stumped...

I was all set on making a good meal tonight. I pulled out my German cookbook and looked up how to make a very basic potato dish as a side to pork cutlets with curry sauce (Okay, curry is not so German; but my Doctor said I need as much curry as possible), and cauliflower as the vegetable to round off the plate.

When I was in the middle of cooking, my younger son, Lucas, walked into the kitchen. Now Lucas is much more likely to try new foods than his older brother. He carefully approached the stove, looked thoroughly at the various pots and pans and then asked: "Where's the good stuff?"

Day 14 – *Feeling of the Day*: Perplexed

No way, could it really be this easy?

It's been two weeks now since I started my new diet, but I made a booboo last night. I got hungry after I came home late at night, around 10:30pm and I know better than eating at that time, especially raw foods like fruits and vegetables.

As I learned recently, if you eat raw foods too close to bedtime, they do not get digested well enough. Then the body goes into rest mode and the foods turn partially into this cheap kind of alcohol that does not sit well in the stomach and can cause sleep disruption.

Well, I ate watermelon because I did not want to eat empty cracker calories, and sure enough, I slept horribly!

I woke up several times with a slight sore throat feeling, just enough to know that something in my body wasn't happy! I could not swallow well. Then I had to go pee in the middle of the night, which is never fun ☹

My husband woke up, too, from my tossing and turning and kept asking me if I was getting sick.

And THEN: When I finally wake up in the morning, one of my finger joints hurt again.

I recalled that it used to hurt quite a bit every morning and throughout the day! I kept stretching it and wanting to 'pop' the joint. And right then, I realized that my finger had not hurt this past week – at all!

I never felt my finger joint this past week hurting from the arthritis that I thought I had! How about that?!?!!

Is this in my head? Or is there really, truly a connection? Could this kind of reaction happen this fast?

I'm still wondering.

And I won't eat late tonight!

Day 16 – *Feeling of the Day*: Grossed out

I tried fake cheese with my no-ingredient bread (aka rice flour bread) last night. No Bueno!!

Just so you know, the fake vegan, gluten-free, no nuts or seeds cream cheese tastes like rubber. In contrast, the fake parmesan has a distinct, full-bodied cardboard flavor!

The fake provolone is doable, as long as I don't think of it as cheese. It's something I can add as a small side to wherever cheese would normally go.

Never eating cardboard cheese again!

But now, I have a moral dilemma! What do I do with the fake cheeses that I simply cannot keep in my refrigerator for a year? Do I throw them away? What about the starving kids in Africa? Do I take the cheeses back to the store? Then they will just throw them away.

Should I pass it on to the neighbor whose daughter is vegan? They might think I'd want to kill her with cardboard. What would I even say? "This is gross, so you can have it."?!? Not very neighborly!

I wish I knew the protocol!

Day 19 – *Feeling of the Day*: Grown-up and proud

I feel like a grown-up! I went to the store and bought raw lentils, so I have to soak them tonight in order to make my Mom's recipe of lentil soup tomorrow. And I went to the butcher's counter at the market to get sausages that will go into the soup!

This is the first time in my life that I will be making soup other than from a package. I know this is terrible, but hey, when I first started writing, I did tell you that I wasn't a cook, right?!?

Well, I wasn't kidding…

The butcher was very friendly in making recommendations as to which sausage might go well with the soup, and he took me seriously, as if this was a normal thing to do! I walked away at least one foot taller than when I had gone into the store!

Feeling slightly anxious but excited to try and have homemade soup to dish out tomorrow night.

This is my third week of the official diet, and I have to admit that I am not really satisfied with the food. I am not looking forward to eating; it is no longer fun, and I have long banished the word 'indulge' from my vocabulary.

But it is a lot of fun to not have pain in my finger all day long! It is also lots of fun to feel my waistline firming up. Even though I did not feel overweight when I started this endeavor, I often felt bloated after a meal, especially when eating out. Not so much now!

So, every time I get tempted to sneak that bite of milk chocolate in, I picture my gut that needs some healing. Then I don't want to burden it with food that is just not going to do me any good. At least for right now.

Well, in any case, since I have broken into the third week, the countdown from 50-something weeks went down to the 49th week! No longer looking at the big 5 in front. That's something.

Day 21 – *Feeling of the Day*: Can't do anything right!

How do you clean up a large amount of burned lentil mush?

I really did it. I managed to burn my lentil soup AND turn it into the least attractive food you would ever want to have in your kitchen!!

It all started well. I soaked the lentils the night before and started cooking in time for last night's dinner. While the lentils simmered, I cut some potatoes, poked the sausages, and seasoned the lentils. After about 45 minutes of simmering, I added the rest of the ingredients for the whole thing to simmer another 30 minutes or so. At least, that's what Mom's recipe called for.

After I added all the ingredients, I left to take Lucas to soccer, while instructing my husband who was already home, to turn off the stove at a certain time and cover the pot. He did everything I asked for, but when I got home from soccer practice an hour later, I opened the door and could smell immediately that something wasn't right with my soup!

I lifted the cover and got that sinking feeling again. It had looked so good at the time when I left for soccer, just the way it was supposed to be! But now... oh dear, a grey mush stared at me, and when I stirred the pot, some of the burned parts moved upwards...

It was no good! ☹

Although it looked as if there were some lentil soup layers that would have been okay – maybe – at least the sausages would be edible, but this was not what I had hoped for! AT ALL!!

My older son, Aaron, fled the scene under the pretense that he had to get to football practice. My husband vanished, too, having to drive said son to practice and then go straight to his evening class.

Lucas and I looked at each other and then looked at the pot. Cheerfully, I called out, "Dinner!"

I served a couple of plates, assuring Lucas that, since the other two had left, the two of us would get to eat all the sausages.

Lucas ate several spoonfuls of the soup and ate the whole sausage. I ate some soup but didn't really like the sausage. After this, Lucas looked at me and said, "I'm sorry, but this is not really that good."

I answered, "I know! This is not really what it was supposed to be like! I promise, I'll make it again and I'll make it right!"

Lucas: "Oh no, it's okay! Don't make it again!"

Since Lucas had been so good about trying the soup, I went ahead and made him mac & cheese for the real dinner.

Tonight's menu: Let's see if I can make tacos!

Day 22 – *Feeling of the Day*: Hungry!

Fooooood! I need food! I'm so hungry! In my attempt to create a dinner menu plan for the week, I forgot that I would also need to have lunch!

So, what do I have? Hmm, there are wheat tortillas for the boys in the fridge, eggs, cheese, ingredients for tonight's dinner, an extremely small portion of leftover veggies that I made the day before yesterday – not enough!

So, protein shake it is!

I wonder if a protein shake tastes good with a side of corn chips???

Day 23 – *Feeling of the Day*: Victorious

YESSSS!!! Total taco success! I followed the recipe on the seasoning package to prepare the ground beef, hand-shredded some lettuce, cut tomatoes into adorable little pieces. Then I put all these toppings into various bowls so that everybody could help themselves to create their own piece of dinner art. Corn tortillas for me, wheat for everybody else.

I also added some pre-packaged guacamole. Pre-packaged for a specific reason. Southern California is not only experiencing a severe drought, but also a severe avocado shortage. And I didn't want to risk buying super-expensive avocados and then have the guacamole turn out mediocre because of my lack of kitchen skills. So, I found the perfect compromise – pre-packaged Guac!

Ready for dinner!

At first, Aaron thought the wheat tortillas were too large and therefore not the right kind. I offered to cut a smaller circle out of the center of the tortilla to make it the right size. He thought that was not going to help the fact that it would taste wrong because it was not the right kind to begin with. Smart child! I should have not engaged in so many discussions with him when he was growing up... My life would be easier now.

Well, after assembling and tasting their first bite, everybody agreed that it was edible, and in fact, quite good! The boys ate multiple tacos, and even I was pleasantly surprised. Aaron rated the taco dinner a 7 out of 10!

A happy ending to this day! And this dish will make it back onto my dinner menu another week!

Day 26 – *Feeling of the Day*: Rejoicing in vain

"Zu Früh Gefreut!"

This is German for a situation in which you rejoiced or celebrated something just a little too soon, and then something goes wrong.

Well, I wrote about a week ago that I felt my waistline firming up and was enjoying that. But now, I find that a distinct fluffiness is creeping back onto my belly. That initial slim down may have just been the result of my ignorance and utter loss at what I could even eat at all, and therefore, I didn't eat much in the beginning.

Now that I have been hanging out at health food stores like other people hang out at the mall, I have found quite a few snacks and foods that will hold me over and fill me up so that I don't get cranky anymore.

But I guess, even though these snacks are more user-friendly (for my particular digestive system) than a handful of salted nuts, I realized that potato chips are not going to make me skinny in the long run.

Fine!! Off to find other snacks!

Day 27 – *Feeling of the Day*: Bloated

Last night I broke down and had some milk chocolate with almonds—BUT, it wasn't my fault! Really!

This is how it happened: I was sitting on the porch with a very large Halloween dish on my lap, filled with chocolates of all varieties. I was supposed to hand them out to cute or scary neighborhood kids upon their begging.

It was not my fault; I didn't even buy this chocolate!

I just happened to finish up my candy-collecting tour with Lucas and then joined our neighbors on their porch who were handing out candy from there. One of our elderly neighbors was sitting with them but decided right then and there that she was done for the night and I should take her place.

Specifically, her place with HER candy! She handed me the bowl and went home peacefully, trusting in my judgment and assuming I was dealt an oversized amount of self-control. Well, I had left that one at home.

Feeling heavy this morning and possibly delayed in my healing process, but I will go back to non-food today and search for that self-control. I know I left it here somewhere.

Day 28 – *Feeling of the Day*: Hopeful, and then headachy

Rejoice, there is hope! I had a wonderful book club meeting last night with wonderful women who all bring wonderful food – not for me now! Well, it turns out that a garlic spread that is sold at the health food chain store nearby is permissible and very tasty with plantains. I never knew!!

Fortunately, all the ladies enjoyed the garlic spread immensely, so we all stank up the home of our gracious hostess together. It was lovely. ☺

In addition to the dip revelation, I found that one of my fellow book-reading club members, Olivia, is also going through a one-year repair phase diet and has to cut out gluten completely. I AM NOT ALONE!!!

It was very nice to be able to commiserate, although she has a great sense of humor that keeps her alive, too. That and beef with vegetables.

We did not have enough time to talk about all the ins and outs of the foodless life because the book discussion took over, but I am sure there's a lot more to come! I have hope!

...later in the afternoon –

I have a migraine! It's a bad day.

It's probably not the food though. The temperature increased from 70 degrees to 83 degrees within one day and the air feels stuffy. I always get knocked out by that type of weather.

Going to bed early at 8:30pm; hubby is taking care of the boys. I can hear them talk until 10pm; that's too late!

It's not good... ☹

Day 29 – *Feeling of the Day*: Frustrated

Hubby had hernia surgery today. He posted a 'Before' selfie on social media from the pre-op room and had 68 comments after he woke up from the anesthesia an hour later!! Why is THAT so interesting? He is only dealing with this for about one hour and has to take it easy for a week with mild pain today and possibly tomorrow. It was a very small hernia; size of a quarter, maybe.

And then one week basically doing nothing, but no more real pain.

I am on week four of my suffering and doing plenty of it, thank you very much!

Sorry to my dear reader, I'm just a tad frustrated today. I love my hubby and am glad everything went so well. ☺

Back to my friend Olivia from the book club. It was not all good news. She told me last night that beans and other legumes are not really your friend either when it comes to healing a leaky gut; in fact, they might make matters worse. So apparently these are not the best source of protein for me to rely on.

Now, I no longer have rice and beans either as a protein source, just rice. Not much of protein right there.

Sooooo, by the end of this diet year, I will be majorly constipated and probably develop a hernia the size of a football. Then, I hope to get at least 71 comments regarding that surgery!!!

Way to look at things optimistically!

Day 30 – *Feeling of the Day*: Annoyed

My face is breaking out. Now I have wrinkles AND pimples! Who says, you can't have it all?!?!?!?!!

After nearly one month of cleansing my system, it seems that my skin has an issue with it and wants some nutrients back that I have dropped out of my diet.

I strongly believe that this breakout is based on an acute lack of milk chocolate in my blood stream. I just know it!

Day 31 – *Feeling of the Day*: Husband is feeling threatened

My husband feels genuinely threatened by my gluten-free soy sauce packages. I admit I might have overdone it a little. My friend Sarah showed them to me the other day. She had a few of those small packages that are usually included in the take-out sushi, but hers were gluten-free.

She said she has been eating gluten-free for a few years now, and always takes these packages along so that she can eat out and not compromise her diet.

I wanted some of those. After scouting out several health food stores in my vicinity, I found that the stores didn't carry the packages at all or discontinued carrying them. So, I ordered online.

Unfortunately, the online source with the best price that I found was a supplier for restaurants, and I now have a box of 200 gluten-free soy sauce packages in my kitchen. I need to make space for them.

Hubby thinks that I have 1,000 packages, so he suggested that we eat sushi almost every single day now, so that we can use up those packages before the year is over.

The only ones happy about the box were my two boys. They loved the strange sensation of digging their hands deep down between the packages. Really, I'm happy about the box, too! Just that I must eat sushi everyday now (for as long as hubby is around)! Funny to think how much I missed sushi when I was pregnant.

Day 32 – *Feeling of the Day*: Excited

It's official! I have survived exactly one month on my new diet!!! I am so excited; I have logged over 30 days of weird food, put my boys through dinner experiments that were gluten-free, half vegan and otherwise new in combinations. I have made it through 1/12th of the assigned time period and reached the first milestone! It is time to celebrate! ☺

Not with food – in case you were thinking I would cheat – maybe I'll light a candle.

Tonight's dinner will be hamburgers (without the bun for me, without the veggies for the picky boys). I will add baked sweet potato fries. That's the plan anyway. I've never made hamburgers from scratch, but I do have meat and I do have seasoning, so I hope this won't go wrong.

Other than that, it's another day with steep increase in temperature, which equals another headache. I took a pill and went to lie down for a while. Just as the pain subsided, my friend Amy called. We both love our coffee and love it even more when we have it in each other's company.

We plan to get together next week, but she doesn't know about this journey of mine yet. Should I bring my own soy creamer? Or should I just try to have coffee with sweetener and no fantastically foamed milk from her home milk frother? Can you froth soy milk?

So many questions! I wonder if coffee will ever taste good again. ☹

Day 33 – *Feeling of the Day*: Mixed up

Ha!! Election Day. The heat is rising, literally! It was 58 degrees this morning when the boys left for school and it's supposed to spike to 88 today! Then back down overnight and tomorrow, expecting a high of 94 degrees!!

Hamburgers last night were a medium success. Hubby helped make the meat but was much faster than the fries in the oven, so we had hamburgers first, and then fries about 20 minutes later.

Note to self: Work on timing.

But the boys ate up, so it must have been okay. The real dessert, chocolate pudding (for the boys only), was a hit and I celebrated my ONE MONTH mark by watching an SNL election special all by myself. Super funny!!!

Another note to self: Always end my thoughts on a good note! ☺

This afternoon I stopped by the store and noticed that I have developed a compulsive habit of buying everything that fits my limited food criteria list. I'm just so scared that I won't have anything to eat at home and that makes me cranky. So, I read labels and if I can eat it, I buy it!

I now have four different kinds of chips in my house, and just for good measure, I threw in a bag of roasted and salted beans that have replaced my mid-morning snack of mixed nuts.

It also makes for rather interesting combinations for lunch. Today out of sheer panic, I bought salad, veggie rolls from the sushi take-out counter, guacamole, and said bean snack. Then I realized that guacamole is cheaper at the other store, so I put it back. That resulted in my eating blue corn chips without guacamole for my after-lunch snack, since I was still hungry after salad and veggie roll (big surprise!). I almost added the instant miso soup to lunch but left it alone after all. Self-control!!

I did, however, try the fake chocolate cake. Not what I was hoping for, but then, I really do appreciate all those people who are trying so hard to make tasty food out of nothing and trying to help people like me!

Please don't stop trying! I would be absolutely lost without those marvelous, health-conscious cooks, bakers and others who have such wonderful and yet, slightly frightening, ideas of making milk out of pea protein. Don't ever stop! I need you!!!

Day 34 – *Feeling of the Day*: In awe of a new discovery

Crock Pot!! CROCK POT! How did I miss this movement?!?!?!! I just went to the store and checked out crock pots, just because they were sitting next to the items I was really looking at.

… and ended up reading the crock pot cookbook from start to finish, until the friendly store assistant reminded me that this was not a library. Well, fine then. I noted down the title of the book, which just so happened to be on sale, to remind myself that this one had a good number of recipes that would work for me. Now, I just need the crock pot to go with it.

While running several errands with hubby (who is still recovering from his surgery, therefore available and bored), we went to the home goods store and decided on a pot that looked pretty and was quite cheap. If anything, this will just be another experiment on my part. Not sure if the boys will be as excited as I am.

Next: Go back to store #1 and actually buy the cookbook. Hubby pointed out that I would find an endless number of recipes online… quite modern, that one, isn't he?!? But I just like a good old-fashioned book with pictures that tell me what my food should look like after it's done!

Tomorrow morning, I will get ingredients for a savory beef stew, which includes potatoes, carrots, and onions. This will be our dinner. I can't wait! Yay for food that is real and therefore nutritious to my children, and at the same time an easy dinner for a busy evening tomorrow night.

Day 35 – *Feeling of the Day:* **Happy with myself**

The crock pot dinner was so easy to make, it was everything I hoped for! The prep work was extremely short and easy, the house smelled so good towards the finish of cooking time, the food was already done whenever we were ready to eat, it was great!

Except the family reaction!

Aaron was gracious by asking if I could just go back to making the things they like to eat, so that I would not have to put so much work into making all these strange new foods. He started to get somewhat grouchy though, when I pointed out that he only likes his Korean ramen noodles. Lucas started laughing, but I silenced him with a stern look and five words: "French fries and fish sticks!"

I guess, it's ok to make those foods sometimes, but it had gotten a little out of hand and thus, my effort to really turn these boys into healthy eaters before college strikes and they must feed themselves. My boys making their own food choices? Scary!

They did, however, eat all the meat parts in the stew, and I was satisfied. After all, I know it takes a while to acquire the taste for certain things. Hubby ate without commenting but took a second serving. I took that as a good sign.

Until later at night, he asked me very carefully if I intended to keep the crock pot. "Not because the food wasn't good, don't get me wrong!" he said. "But just considering the size of that thing versus the limited space in our kitchen!" Hm, how do I take this? I chose to go along with it and be happy with my cooking effort!

Day 36 – *Feeling of the Day*: Contemplating ideas

Sushi lunch with hubby.

Maybe I need to start learning how to make sushi myself. It would be a lot cheaper in the long run!

Hmmmm, nah! That's scary. I like fish, but it must be shrink-wrapped when I first acquire it.

Day 38 – *Feeling of the Day*: Slightly hopeful

Lucas's soccer team suffered a loss today during play-offs, which eliminated them from the final tournament. Devastating and unexpected, especially since they had done so well up until today. So, in order to comfort the boys after the mood had taken a nosedive, we got to eat a simple and tasty lunch: Rice with kimchee and hotdog. Manageable, things are looking up.

This week I noticed that my gums were inflamed for a couple of days on the upper right-hand side. I've been experiencing this every now and then ever since I had a dental procedure done about two years ago. At the time I got a really bad infection on the tooth that was being treated, and I was sick for three weeks with extreme pain, swelling of the gums, headaches, fevers etc.

The doctors were never able to tell me what that really was, and it passed. However, I still get the same inflammation every now and then in a much milder version. Sometimes, it may last for a week. But this time, it lasted only for two days or so.

Is this due to some healing taking place? Or just because there was no more inflammation to be had? Not sure, but I'll take it either way.

Rob and I are going out to a classical concert tonight and will probably have sushi for dinner on the way. I feel as if I am running out of ideas.

Day 39 – *Feeling of the Day*: Worried, things are going backwards

No sushi dinner yesterday. I barely had time for a little snack before we left. It was pretty late after the concert and the only place that was still open was one of those 24-hour diners with the anti-health menu. There were exactly two items that I could have eaten. My first choice was minestrone, but they were already out. So, I was left with a side of French fries!

Seriously!! I had a plate full of French fries as a late-night dinner. I am starting to doubt that I ever knew the slightest bit about healthy eating considering that this is the best possible choice for me!

My healthy diet is taking a turn for the worse! The night before last we had gone out to the movies with some friends and all the kids, dinner at the food court to follow. My best choice was broccoli beef and rice from the Chinese fast food. I'm not liking the direction this is going.

So, today I need to turn my meals back around towards the pure and nutritious choices I had made in the beginning of this journey – Sushi lunch!!

I believe I have now used a whopping five packs of my 200-pack shipment. Only 11 months and 195 gluten-free soy sauce packs to go!

Day 40 – *Feeling of the week*: Pressured to do it all

After about four weeks of this experiment, I did lose some weight after all. I am sure it's a combination of several factors:

- No dairy
- Less mindless snacking
- Less chocolate, etc.
- I'm also really not excited about food anymore

At the lowest point, it looked as if I had lost about six pounds from my average weight before, but I've gained a couple back after I invested heavily in fast food rather than my home-cooked experiments.

I noticed that my body shape has not really changed. Although lighter, my little belly pooch is still there. So, in essence, I have just simply shed one protective layer! Everything else is the same.

All this suffering and no flat abs! Is the universe sending me a sign that I really do need to work out more specifically if I want to make a difference there?!??

Well, maybe... I'll think about it. I know I'm supposed to do weight bearing exercise anyway to keep my bones strong before menopause hits and all hell breaks loose (or at least all bones break loose).

But I should also stretch for at least 15 minutes a day, lay on the giant rubber ball for another twenty minutes a day to reverse all this hunching over, do my neck exercise to regain the curve in my spine, I should read the news, read a book with my kids, have meaningful conversations over dinner, sleep at least eight hours, take a bath before bedtime for better sleep quality, stop watching TV at least one hour before bed, visit my elderly neighbor who is sick, drink eight glasses of water, call my parents, my niece and my brother more often, do some cardio, have date night with my husband, and voilà: I filled 36 hours in my day! Not to mention the things that I would just simply LIKE to do.

And that's all besides working, running the household, raising the boys and, well, I guess, we're all in the same boat. I don't need to rant on any further.

Tonight's dinner: Black bean pasta. I'm already nervous. it's not pasta with black beans, but pasta made with black bean flour. The fusilli actually are black! Found this beauty at the local market today after mindless browsing. Will report back tomorrow!

Day 41 – *Feeling of the Day*: Disgusted!

Eeeewwww! Don't ever try black bean pasta, unless you want to hurt your inner Italian!

Or change your attitude to not expect pasta, but black beans, which I probably should have done. Who thinks 'pasta' anyway, when you're cooking black beans, even in fusilli format?! I guess the joke is on me!

However, by the end of the meal, I had come to terms with the taste and it wasn't as bad as when I first tasted the bean noodle to see if it was al dente. When are beans ever al dente, unless undercooked? In any case, I will go back to rice pasta or corn meal pasta. Those were actually pretty good.

I also realized that I completely forgot to make my weekly dinner plan! No plan, no dinner! It went completely over my head this weekend, and now, I'm in limbo. Gotta make a plan right now and really quick.

Tonight is high school orientation night for Aaron, so dinner will be a 'wing-it' situation.

Thursday, I have no idea!

Friday eating leftovers and

Saturday leaving for a road trip (that'll be interesting)!!

There: My dinner plan is done! ☺

Day 42 – *Feeling of the Day*: Full of experimental spirit

Dinners this week are coming along beautifully according to plan (see above). After high school orientation night yesterday, it was way too late to even think about cooking at home, so we picked up pizza for the boys. I had some more of my pasta shaped black beans with tomato sauce. I'm seriously over it now! There is more left, but I might secretly make it disappear. Stealth grinding!

Today was interesting: There was a 'no idea' on the dinner plan, so I decided to make regular (aka wheat) pasta for the boys and add a veggie stir-fry to use up all the fresh vegetables before leaving for our trip.

I cut up the bell pepper and zucchini then fried it in coconut oil. I'm allowed the oil, although nothing else of the coconut. I seasoned the veggies with Italian seasoning, and then thought, well, what about some curry on that? Curry and coconut go well together, right?! So, I added the curry and stirred and fried away happily.

You know how little kids, when they first start coloring, tend to use all the colors in all the places and in the end their creation is all mixed into one indistinct brown piece of art?

Well, that's what happened to my stir-fry after adding pretty much all the seasonings I own. It tasted the equivalent of a two-year old's painting.

However, Hubby came to the rescue just as I finished the stir-fry. He brought home a couple of his friends from work and suggested that we go out to dinner together. I obliged!

But now, I know, I did wrong again. We went back to our favorite little Greek restaurant and I ordered the veggie kabob. The seasoning on this was very well balanced!

I also had some fries and a salad on the plate, and sure enough, I did eat the raw salad, although I know better than this. No raw foods after 4pm! I should have stopped myself, should have, should have, should have!!

Now, I feel very full. To make up for it, we went on to have coffee, and to help the digestion, I had a double shot of espresso – with sugar in it!

Man, I'm going to get a lot of work done tonight!!!

Or, maybe I should take care of myself, relax and watch an episode or two of TV drama? No! I should not! That won't be good for my sleep. But hey, I already messed up. I feel as if things are not going the way they should. I really need to go back to purism!

I'm worried about our upcoming trip!

Still Day 42, Midnight – Oh, midnight already, I should probably go to bed! Although I'm not tired, but I know I need my sleep!

Day 43 – 12:20am – Ready for bed after a bit of dawdling; but wait, I need to write one more email and confirm something on my calendar. Then I'll go to bed!

1 am: I can't sleeeeeeep! I'm not tired but I'll just lay here and wait.

1:25am: I can't sleep, I need to… (zzzzzzzzzz)

2:35 am: Hubby comes home and wakes me up! I'm awake!! That means, I slept for a little, but now, I'm awake! (zzzzzzzz)

6:30am (alarm rings): Nooooooooooooooooooo!! Snooze!

6:35am: Arrgh! Snooze!

6:38am: Fiiiiine! Ok then, getting up! Can't have the boys be late for school!

Day 43 - midmorning – *Feeling of the Day:* No time to think about my feelings

Panicked before our trip, I raided the health food store to stock up on food items that will last me for one week. We are leaving tomorrow, going to Oregon to stay in one of our timeshares that we have never visited before. I understand it's in a very, very small town. Apparently, there's only one grocery store, and I assume it's not a health food store.

We picked this location because:

a) we have never been to Oregon with the family,

b) I really like the outdoors and need a fix of lush green, and

c) because this was the only location with availability on a short notice.

The timeshare unit typically includes a nice little kitchen, so we'll be cooking for ourselves, unless there is a restaurant in said small town. So, I needed to make sure I'll have enough food for myself to eat. The boys and Rob will always find something; I'm not worried about them.

When I looked at my shopping cart though, I realized that I was leaning heavily towards cookies, dark chocolates and salty snacks. Maybe, I should include some lunch and dinner foods as well. I picked a couple of cans of lentil soup, split pea soup and a pack of rice pasta. I should be good.

Better not forget to take along some of my gluten-free soy sauce packs as well. You never know!

While at the store, I asked the sales assistant if I could use ghee, clarified butter, to bake. I remembered that doc told me I could use the pure oils of milk, coconut etc. in my diet, because they don't contain any of the proteins that I seem to be sensitive to. And in my head, I am getting ready for the holidays, still thinking that I might be able to bake some Christmas cookies with modified recipes.

The sales assistant didn't know, so she asked another helper. He knew that ghee is better for you than butter but wasn't sure how to use it for baking. They asked me to try it out and then report back.

I have the best of intentions! But no baking until after our trip.

Looking at my current food intake, I get the feeling that I should probably cut down on sugar as well. It just doesn't seem right to continue eating sugar when I'm trying to heal my gut. Ugh, this is going to be more difficult.

I already replaced my afternoon coffee including its variations of non-dairy vanilla milk with a cup of tea yesterday. I feel so British!! And it wasn't bad, but this afternoon I was really looking forward to that coffee. Maybe, I'll just do some slow adjustments, cutting some of the sweets. I won't do such a radical cut like I did with the doctor's list. Hmm, sounds reasonable at least.

5pm: I need a nap after last night's sleep disaster.

8pm: All packed, going to bed for early morning departure, around 5am to beat traffic out of the LA area. Yay, vacation!!

Day 44 – *Feeling of the Day*: Out of my comfort zone

Day 1 of Road Trip – We left at 5:30am. We're having our first break with breakfast in the middle of nowhere at Del Taco. I'm not sure this is what Doc had in mind for my diet change.

Lunch was at another middle of nowhere; halfway through California we found a little town with an Italian restaurant, self-serve with a good selection of sandwiches etc. I got to have minestrone soup and picked out the pasta from it. To make up for the loss of solids, I also got three slices of prosciutto. I don't know if I'm doing this thing right, this whole elimination diet.

Also, due to lack of silverware, I ate the prosciutto with my fingers. I feel so out of my element; this is just not me!

Coffee on the go was a double whammy! We stopped by the supermarket about two to three hours before arrival in order to get water, some food for the boys and hubby (I almost forgot that they need food, too!)

I was craving my afternoon coffee, so I went to the coffee kiosk inside the supermarket. The slightly overwhelmed barista took my order for a small soy cappuccino and a cup of hot water for hubby. I paid for the cappuccino, soy milk and hot water, $4.20. Meanwhile, she had started the water flow for hot water, the cup overflowed, and barista had to run back to make it stop. She placed the cup into a second cup, because the water was extremely hot, handed it to me with a smile and said: "Have a nice day!"

I looked at her expectantly, and she remembered: "Oh yeah, your cappuccino! Coming right up!" Cheery as ever, she proceeded to foam the milk and stir up that coffee drink. Lucas wanted some of the foamed milk, so he stole a few tastes before I added my sugar and then took it to the car. It was pouring rain, so we all hurried to load the groceries, get in and go.

I took a sip of the coffee: It wasn't soy milk...

Because I really, really needed that pick up, I allowed myself a few sips, but it turned out that I actually didn't like the milky taste of regular milk as much!

Get that? Now coffee is definitely ruined for me forever! No version seems to be right anymore!

Day 45 – *Feeling of the Day*: Oblivious

We had reached our destination at 7pm the night before: Klamath Falls, OR. Beautiful! The town is bigger than expected. I might find food here!

I don't remember what I ate, though. I'm on vacation!

Day 46 – *Feeling of the Day*: Ignorant

It's freezing cold! We crossed over the mountain pass to get to Ashland today. On the way we pulled over so the boys could play in the snow. The car promptly got stuck in the snow and drifted towards the ditch when trying to get back on the road.

After a little back and forth, we realized that we weren't going to get out by ourselves. Thank goodness it was midday and we waived at a couple of cars. Two cars stopped to help; the third driver just waived back at us.

The first question the friendly Oregonian asked us was, "You don't have a four-wheel drive?"

"?? Ummm, no."

"You don't have a shovel?"

"?? Ummmmmmmm, no."

We are new and so very ignorant about the 'pulling over into the snow bank' thing, but I'll make a note of adding 'shovel' to my standard packing list when I get home!

Arriving in Ashland without any further incidents, I had a sushi lunch!

Day 47 – *Feeling of the Day*: Frozen!

Early morning adventure today. Lucas had wanted to go fishing with the early birds, but it was snowing when we woke up. We decided we'd still give it a try since we had nothing else to do.

After collecting all the accessories and necessities and scraping snow and ice bits off the car, we all climbed into the car to go drive to the lake's shore on the resort property. The helpful gentleman at the front desk had told us the night before that the good fishing spot was only going to be a one-minute drive. But if someone says, "One minute", I'd assume at least three to four minutes.

Ha! I'm not THAT naive!

The slipping and sliding with the car started as soon as I pulled out of the parking spot. Déja vu! I backed out very carefully and went back and forth in real short moves, so I wouldn't slide into the car next to us. After I had made it far enough to turn the car straight and pointing downhill, Rob rightfully stated, "This is crazy!! We won't be able to get back up the hill! No chance!!"

So, I slipped and slid ever so gently downhill and into the next available parking spot three cars down. That was that. The end of the journey by car.

Aaron and Lucas were still motivated to go fishing, and I am really excited about reasonably sized hikes, I said, "We'll walk! Can't be too bad if we were only going to drive three to four minutes, can it?!?"

It was a beautiful morning; clear now with occasional snow. The path snaked its way through the extensive resort area (more extensive than we knew!). I took some pictures; then my phone froze. Rob's phone had already given up, but who cares? We found deer and rabbit traces; it's an adventure: Four Californians in the Oregon wilderness (on resort property)!

After about twenty minutes in the cold, however, Lucas started to complain that his legs were hurting. Five minutes later, we actually saw a deer crossing our path! Sheer excitement!!

It was another twenty-five minutes of walking, then Aaron started doubting the validity of the map. I would never have admitted it, but I started wondering, too. How I would get those boys back to the timeshare without Uber (no Uber in the wilderness...!)?

Eventually, we finally made it to the waterfront. It was as if someone had flipped the switch on the mood-meter. Aaron and Lucas were excited to set up their fishing poles and they got right down to business. Rob and I cleared off a log, folded one of the timeshare's towels that Rob had brought (smart move!) and we sat. We watched the crazy kids who came up with the idea of getting up at 7:30am (on vacation!) to go fishing in the snow. Did I mention we are new?

When we finally got so cold that it wasn't even funny anymore, we packed up and started our way back. It was snowing harder now; the wind was sharp, and a fog had set in. Rob tried to coax me into hitch-hiking. I said I would, but we were missing a key ingredient – a car coming our way!

The kids were miserable, and we walked uphill in the snow, carrying loads of gear but no fish, so the mood had tanked. But then: Aaahh, a car!!

All four of us tried to look desperate and yet likeable, excited to see the car and at the same time pitiful. It worked!

The car came to a stop right in front of us. A very nice couple sat in it, the driver rolled down the window and looked at us. In my most shaky voice, I said, "We are so cold and we need to get to our timeshare."

Their eyebrows rose way up and, although the first question was not "You don't have a shovel?", it sounded much like it, only slightly different, "You are walking?!?!?!!"

"... Errr, yes...."

Well, the driver told us to hop in and off we went, riding back to our place! What a relief!! After our faces had defrosted, we were able to engage in a very pleasant conversation with the driver and his wife. It was NOT a three to four-minute drive! More like fifteen minutes or so.

We got back into our place around 11:30am and had not had breakfast yet, since the original plan had only included a short drive, about an hour worth of fishing and the quick drive back. Now, we were hungry, and I ate my dinner leftovers from the past two nights! It turns out that lentil soup and super-grain pasta is so very good together – when you're really hungry!

I started missing fresh veggies. I've been winging my meals during this trip – from Mexican take-out (corn tostada with beef and lettuce) to sushi to bun-less burgers with fries. But I couldn't do it much longer. I need veggies! Soon!!

This afternoon we stopped by the supermarket and found white asparagus! This is the only kind I knew growing up, so I was very excited. I promptly bought three packs for Rob and myself. I can't believe it, but on the way out of the market, these words came out of my mouth: "I'm really looking forward to the asparagus!"

Who says stuff like that??

Day 49 – *Feeling of the Day*: In pain

Ah, Thanksgiving Day!! I woke up at 4am with a splitting headache! I don't know what caused it, and there are way too many variables to consider:

- I may not have eaten the right thing (most likely!)
- I may not have eaten in time
- I may have been dehydrated because in the cold, I did not remember to drink enough
- I may have exhausted myself, because after our early morning fishing adventure, we ran errands in the afternoon; and on top of that, went ice skating thereafter. It was a lot of fun, but maybe a little too much
- I may have stressed over the vacation planning that we had done over the last few days, trying to get everyone's approval for next year's plans, which proves to be more and more difficult
- I may have carried that into my sleep and then been grinding my teeth

Whatever it was that caused it, it was no good! I took a homeopathic pill at 4am, then half a regular pill at 5am, tried to sleep some more. Repeat of the treatment at 8am and 9am. The boys went fishing yet again with Rob, and I stayed behind to get some more sleep.

At 11:30am, they came back to check in with me. Lucas stayed (and watched TV while looking after me). Aaron and Rob went out again to try and catch some more fish. It didn't work. In fact, they did not catch a single thing during the whole trip, so Aaron started to lose fishing motivation. ☹ Understandable!!

They returned yet again at 12:30pm to see if I was up for lunch. Although Lucas and I had eaten a small breakfast together, I was getting a little better and thought it would be a nice to go out no matter what.

Thank goodness we're traveling on Thanksgiving Day this year. Had we been celebrating in traditional style, I would have had to cut out the turkey, stuffing, mashed potatoes, pumpkin pie and all other desserts! I'd be left with hardly anything. Probably just green beans without gravy. Not a pretty picture!

So instead, we headed back to the Black Bear Diner where the bun-less burger, fries and dressing-free salad was a solid meal that I would be able to enjoy. When we got to Black Bear, we found that we were not the only ones without the family gathering this day, and the diner was actually serving proper Thanksgiving dinner with your choice of turkey or ham!

Well, ham it is! It came with all the sides as they should be. I asked if I could substitute mashed potatoes with fries, which made the waitress cringe just ever so slightly. After I explained that I could not have dairy, she gave me a sad, but warm smile, and I felt all better.

Today, being a holiday, I might put real creamer into my coffee, or alternately, I might have a piece of milk chocolate, or I might have a bite of the apple pie that comes with the meal. I'm dreaming!

Note to self: Don't have Doc read my notes!

Day 50 – *Feeling of the Day*: Sad to leave

Friday, we are leaving Klamath Falls. This time, we are breaking up the drive into two days, stopping over by our friends in Danville, CA.

Food choices TBD.

Day 52 – *Feeling of the Day*: Travel aftermath, just busy!

Back home, I was able to make very safe food choices today. It is the first Sunday of Advent today, which we usually celebrate by lighting one of four candles in an Advent wreath during afternoon coffee time. It usually goes along with abundant sweets, but this did not happen today. Unpacking, laundry and fixing the car happened instead.

Funny thing, my flesh seems stronger than my mind: I was ready to allow myself a small chocolate bar or regular cookie in order to mark this special day, but the entire family was all over the place today and never came together for a meal.

So, I let it go and am now looking forward to next Sunday, the second Sunday of Advent, when I will allow myself some chocolate or a regular cookie.

Day 53 – *Feeling of the Day*: **Encouraged**

Dinner plan? What dinner plan...?? Today is the first day back to school after Thanksgiving break, and to me that means Christmas time has begun – I am making a cookie plan! ☺

I looked up two or three Christmas cookie recipes that I might be able to modify, using gluten-free flour, etc. I made sure I looked for recipes that don't require eggs or milk, because I just don't want to substitute too many ingredients. It's enough to write my diet notes; I don't want to write a cookbook on top of that! With my luck, that would be some book, with not much useful stuff in there.

So, I asked again at this other store if one can bake with ghee instead of butter, and finally, one of the sales clerks looked at me and said: "Well, yes! That is what it's made for!! Don't use it as a spread on your bread, it's yucky!"

Delighted, I paid the exorbitant price for having gluten-, dairy-, egg-, and wheat-free cookies! Well, I don't have the cookies yet. I must try to bake them, maybe tomorrow, because today is Cyber Monday, and I'm looking for this particular gift for Lucas.

Day 54 – *Feeling of the Day*: Pleasantly surprised

I did it!! I made ghee cookies after a recipe that should have produced almond cookies in the shape of triangles. I substituted butter with ghee, sugar with xylitol, wheat flour with gluten-free all-purpose flour, and milk with vanilla pea milk (only 1 tablespoon anyway), and voila! The cookies came out not tasting too bad!

I split the batch into two smaller batches because I found the dough to be way too sticky and could not form rolls at all. With the first half of the batch I formed roll-like shapes and flattened them so I could later cut them into triangles. I let the dough cool off in the fridge in order to solidify a bit before baking. When I went to bake it, the dough started running immediately and the initial triangle shape was lost. The cookies spread to irregular circles, but I won't discriminate. It's all good.

I used the second batch to form rolls again; however, I added a little more flour. I accidentally used rye flour because I grabbed the wrong bag. But again, it's edible and even Lucas thinks they are pretty good. Well, not so bad!

The only problem is that they are extremely delicate and crumble into pieces as soon as you touch them. I was thinking of making sandwich cookies by stacking two cookies with some jelly in between, but I am not sure how they are going to hold up. Jelly would add a little more taste, of course, but there might not be much cookie left after I handle them.

I shall try tomorrow.

It's been enough work for the day today, and I had a headache again throughout most of the day. It just started to fade over dinner time, which is unusual. I normally get the headache and it won't go away until the next day.

Got lucky, I guess!

Day 55 – *Feeling of the Day*: Realizing that there are still problems

I am starting to realize that I continue to hurt my body with food that I shouldn't be eating as much, even though it's not on the forbidden list. It's the sugar, green tea (which is on my list), soy creamer almost daily in my coffee, maybe too much rice (in various forms: as pasta, bread, actual rice, as flour in the cookies I eat every day, etc.). Also, dark chocolate, even if it is only one or two small pieces, but again, nearly every day.

This is so embarrassing, but I'm not doing as well as I should! Maybe that's why I still get headaches.

Also, the fast food hiccups during our road trip weren't exactly great, I guess. I'm really struggling. ☹

Hmmmm, I need to reconsider my diet approach. Yet again!!

Day 56 – *Feeling of the Day*: Enraged!

Tonight, a friend came over and tried to tell me that there is no such thing as food allergies! It's all in your head, he says, and there's no scientific proof of any allergies in people at all!! In fact, people only develop an allergic reaction once they know they've consumed a food that they BELIEVE to be allergic to! Otherwise, if they didn't know they are consuming the food, they will not have a reaction! And an allergic reaction would at most be something like diarrhea!!

I couldn't believe it!! I was so upset after this lecture! I had an espresso and three cookies (8pm)!

Well, it's midnight now; I need to get to bed. Oh no, not this again! Didn't I do this before? Late espresso and then sleep issues?

Well, glad to know it's all in my head!

Day 58 – *Feeling of the Day*: Pretty happy

Ghee cookies – double layered with jam in between – are a total success! Everyone's all in! ☺ I mixed some powdered sugar with water to get frosting and poured it in zigzagged stripes across the cookies. Now they look like real Christmas cookies!

I also made my vanilla crescent cookies today that I bake every year. Rob really wanted these, and I made them according to the traditional recipe, no substitutes. But now I have faith in experimenting with the ingredients! Tomorrow I will try that recipe with all my substitutes, and this time, I will replace butter with coconut oil! Ha! Take that, gluten-free vegan bakery!

The only thing I don't know yet how to substitute is the egg yolk. Any ideas? Anybody?

Meanwhile, it's the end of the week and we survived without a dinner plan. I don't know how we survived, but it worked out. Well, I do have a small inkling of an idea: All the leftovers from the fridge are finished, the quick fix frozen dinners for the boys are tapped into, and we went out to eat last night. So, I guess the no-dinner plan works only every now and then.

Tomorrow: More cookie-baking, but also definitely making a dinner plan for this week!

Day 59 – *Feeling of the Day*: Searching for Sushi-company

Haven't had sushi in a while. Experiencing withdrawals. Besides that, I still have about 189 soy sauce packs to go. I need to find a friend to go to lunch with, so I can use up my packs!

Day 60 – *Feeling of the Day*: Baffled

Experiment number two with my vanilla cookies: I looked up egg yolk substitutes online and guess what I found? "It depends"!?!?

It depends on the function of the egg in the recipe! How should I know? How does the egg know what to do when entering the dough??

The egg will apparently either function as leavening, or as a binder, or for moisture. I can follow the moisturizing function; I get that from my night cream for the face in my bathroom cabinet. It's something I can understand. But the other two? How does anyone know? I realize how little I know about food.

Tomorrow I must buy soy lecithin. It's what I am supposed to substitute the egg yolk with. And then, we'll see.

Day 61 – *Feeling of the Day*: Bloated

Today was a day with no vegetables – No Bueno!

I worked in my office until noon. Rob was home and he was so sweet to have lunch ready the moment I was done. He made pasta and a beef/bacon mix, but he made rice especially for me. It was really tasty. ☺

I was hungry, so I ate a good amount, although not outrageous, I thought. Later, we ran errands and had a coffee break in between.

I realized that I was feeling way too full, nearly bloated again, and I anxiously waited for this feeling to pass. It was a distinct heaviness that was dragging me down. And that is exactly how I used to feel when eating out or eating lower quality food.

The beef had been regular supermarket beef, not organic, let alone grass-fed. It had been white rice, and the coffee was, well, it was coffee with soy milk. In addition, I had a large cup of water along with the meal.

I do not miss feeling this way at all! And I don't want to feel this way again, this unnaturally bloated stomach, my tummy out to 'here', and the heavy feeling that makes me slow.

I do not like it at all!!

Also, today is my two-month anniversary of the 'no-food' diet! I am starting to truly appreciate how I feel when I am eating the way I am supposed to!

I look better and my energy level is starting to come up, except for when I stay up until midnight to write these notes.

Okay, I get it! Good night!

Day 62 – *Feeling of the Day*: Up and down, up and down

Ok, here we go again, the rollercoaster of not eating well. Yesterday too full after lunch and coffee. I had a very light dinner to compensate for the heaviness. Then I was hungry late at night because I didn't have enough dinner. I snacked on roasted, salted beans and edamame until I was really full again.

Not good at all!

The next morning, I was still full of beans (now I know how bean bags feel!), so I had a light breakfast only, and then went out to run lots of errands with my best friend Victoria. We had lunch together, and I started feeling better because it was all vegetables.

After lunch we parted ways, and I ran so many more errands that I completely exhausted myself to the point where I thought I was going to keel over while cooking dinner. I made Pasta Asciutta, my Mom's recipe, which is a meat and tomato sauce. It came out really well, and everybody ate up!

But I was soooo tired from being up and running around all day that I had to go to bed at 9:30pm; I didn't feel good at all. ☹

Day 63 – *Feeling of the Day*: Sick

Seriously sick! I woke up with a headache, a little nausea, and general weakness. I think, besides sudden increase in temperature, not eating in time, stressing over my 'To Do list' and stuffy rooms, I have to add 'Seriously Overdoing it in One Day/Not Taking a Break When Needed' to the list of headache triggers.

I took it easy today and starting to feel better this evening, but still exhausted. Where's my bed???

I think I can hear it calling me. Coming!

Day 65 – *Feeling of the Day*: Proud

So proud! We had a Christmas party with neighbors tonight. A potluck where there was plenty of food that was agreeable to Doc's list of my forbidden foods. Although I had a couple of helpings of the soup and some rice and raw veggie sticks, I also dove into the dessert. My own adaptations of traditional Christmas cookies (turned gluten-free and vegan) were welcomed and generally found tasty. I was quite surprised at how well they turned out, and our guests were shocked to find out that these were indeed vegan and gluten-free!

I must say, my adaptation of the vanilla half-moon cookies, lightly dusted with powdered sugar, that I changed to coconut half-moon cookies (due to my using the oil instead of butter), now coated with melted dark baking chocolate really don't resemble the original at all if not for the shape.

If I was to change the shape to a triangle, I could indeed have invented a whole new cookie! Maybe that's what I should do? Take a basic recipe, replace all the evil ingredients, give it a new taste, change the basic shape, and it would be an Annette Original!

How very clever! I am happy with my new-found baking skills! ☺

Also, I strongly resisted the urge to go back for salty late-night snacks, even though I felt a pull extraordinaire towards the pantry. It was very good indeed to simply go brush my teeth instead, just so that the craving disappeared, brushed away in circles with my fabulous electric toothbrush.

Day 66 – *Feeling of the Day*: Food coma

Ughh, vermicelli coma!! Eating out is not my friend!

As part of a visit to a Christmas fair, our family and a few friends decided to go to a Vietnamese restaurant (extremely Christmassy!). I had the vermicelli (very thin rice noodles) with fish sauce and grilled beef, and it came with some fresh cucumber, carrots and salad. All good, except for the fact that this restaurant's food was just not the best quality, I think. Specifically, the meat.

Again, feeling way to full after leaving the restaurant, and if I can't control myself, I am bound for another roller coaster food trip. I really want to try, but tomorrow is the next holiday party to attend – a potluck luncheon with the ladies from my networking group.

I wonder how many more Christmas gatherings I can survive (with slight cheating or less than ideal eating circumstances) without having to add a whole additional month to my 'No-Food' year'??

But to be honest, it was my own fault. I was not very hungry to begin with because I'd had a good-sized lunch in addition to some fruit and cookies in the afternoon with coffee. I really didn't need a whole big dinner. I just ate because it was tasty.

How do I stop myself from eating just because it tastes good, even when I'm not hungry?

New challenge!!

Day 68 – *Feeling of the Day*: Sick with the cold

Dinner plan this week: Everybody fend for themselves. I am sick! Got a bad cold, so I managed to empty some soup from the package into the sauce pan and heat it for myself. Everybody else is on their own. ☹

Day 69 – *Feeling of the Day*: Craving fish sticks

Meal plan for the day: Hot tea with fresh lemon and honey, elderberry juice for my cold, concentrated acai berry juice, water, soup, nose spray, cough drops and gargling with anti-cold essential oil in hot water.

That's about it.

I realize I haven't had fish in quite a while. I seem to be leaning on the beans for protein recently. Last night, when I finally did get down to put fish sticks in the oven for Lucas, I wanted one so badly!! I just wanted that crispy texture with the soft fish inside! When I pulled the tray out of the oven, I could practically taste the fish stick without even touching it!

Ughh, when is this over?!?!?

I know it's been only two months out of twelve, but really, isn't this a pretty good run already? Can't it be the time now that I start to reintroduce foods into my diet that I had eliminated? Can it? Can it, PLEASE??

Later in the afternoon:

I asked (via email) and Doc says "No."

Day 70 – *Feeling of the Day*: Still sick

Man, I'm sick! This is no fun! Last winter I did not have a cold at all, and this year, I am down for the third day now with congestion and aching all over. I am so tired, too!

I ate good stuff for lunch, mixed salad, tofu curry as well as a left-over bean and corn salad. Fruit in the afternoon with a couple of small cookies along with my tea.

I know that is quite the combination, but I didn't care.

I was just so tired because I'd been working in the office all morning, and running errands later, trip to the orthodontist with Aaron, and finally, I was spent! So, when Rob fed the boys dinner, I didn't want to eat; I just wanted to sleep.

Now, Rob has left to go out tonight, and I suddenly craved potato chips. Those turned into my dinner. Not stellar. ☹

I'm full, tired and generally cranky. Going to bed!

Day 71 – *Feeling of the Day*: Grumpy

Oh no, I can't believe this! There is a sushi lunch within reach, and I can't go because I'm still sick! This would have been my chance to go from 189 packs of soy sauce down to maybe 187!! This sucks!

This is what happened. Rob is home today, and suggested we take his parents out to lunch. They live about a 30-minute drive from our house. Normally when we pick them up for lunch, we always go to this fabulous sushi restaurant in Los Angeles' Little Tokyo. I love their food, the quality, the ambience; everything is GOOD about this place! And now, I can't go because I took another pain pill this morning, and my rule is (when applied to anyone in the family): If you are too sick to get up and go to work/school, then you're also too sick to go out and play.

Well, I've been doing very light housework, as in, getting up with the boys and making some breakfast, getting Aaron to school early (it was raining, and then I take the boys by car; I don't make them ride the bike in the rain). Then I had breakfast with Lucas. By the time he should have gone to school, Rob was up so I asked if he could take Lucas because my headache was getting stronger.

Since then, I've been sitting on the couch with water and tea (which I made myself!), called my mom briefly, texted my best friend, listened to Christmas music, and shopped online for Christmas gifts for my overseas family. One present bought so far.

All that has taken all the energy out of me, and now, I'm exhausted and can't go to sushi!

Well, I asked Rob to make me one to go, but of course, it's not the same.

This cold better be over soon!!!

Later, early afternoon:

Take home sushi is no good! The miso soup was cold, but the fish was somewhat warm. Yikes, next time I better go myself!

Day 72 – *Feeling of the Day*: Better, but not as good as I thought

And Phoenix rises from the ashes!!! I got UP from bed, dressed, and stayed up! Although not in perfect condition (lingering cough and congestion), I was even able to take a little walk this morning. It's a perfect day, sunny blue skies, just chilly enough to feel cool air on my cheeks and make me think that it's winter.

When I returned home, I noticed that my front yard needed some help, so I cut back some shrubs and trimmed the little plants. Still not entirely well but doing some gardening! I think this calls for celebration.

Maybe I need to go to the mall? Not that I need any more presents; I am pretty much done, but I do like to wander around the stores with all the decorations and the Christmas music. Since I am not in search for any specific gift, I can enjoy the browsing all on my own!

I have gifts for everyone, but maybe I need something for myself. Think rewarding myself for the discipline I've shown throughout the last two months, twelve days, three hours and twenty-four minutes. Who's counting?

So, off I go, and I solemnly swear that I am up to no good! ;)

Afternoon:

Oh boy! Now, that was wishful thinking. Yesterday, I was still down and out, and today, I should be walking, gardening, AND going to the mall? About five minutes into the drive, I was exhausted. But I carried on, because it was a rare moment of time to myself on the weekend. This never happens, and I was determined to take advantage of it.

And I was prepared. I had brought a newspaper to read while waiting for a parking spot. But I generally have good parking karma, and it worked this time, too. I leisurely entered the mall with a superior air of not needing a thing and walked from one end to the other. In reality, it was not so superior or leisurely, but rather slow and slightly dragging, because the last day of this cold was catching up to me.

I'm also not a great shopper, so instead of trying on any of the cute pieces I saw, I thought to myself, "I could come back for this" and slouched on.

Finally, I went home for a late lunch. Nothing seemed appealing at the mall, the smell of buttery popcorn overdosing me from the moment I had entered.

Well, gotta rest for a bit because we still have a Christmas party to go to tonight!

Day 74 – *Feeling of the Day*: Refreshed

So, I'm back to making my dinner plan for the week. It really does feel better to know what I'll be doing each day, instead of waiting until 6pm, and then trying to produce a decent meal for the boys with whatever it is that I find in the fridge and pantry.

AND I found two new food categories that'll make it much easier to fill the number of days:

1. Leftovers in the fridge
2. Leftovers in the freezer (from those times when I had enough food to consider it a whole other meal for later)

This is brilliant! I already filled two days of the week! I'm going out one more night with my girlfriends, and don't you know it, the week is half done! For the rest of the time, there'll be soup, maybe we'll go out one night, and then there's Christmas Eve with our traditional Hawaii Toast.

This week is done, hooray!

Hawaii toast has been a tradition in my family for as long as I can remember, and it has now blossomed into our tradition as well. It consists of toast (toasted), spread some mayonnaise on it, layer of ham, a pineapple ring and sliced cheese on top, and then bake it in the oven until the cheese melts: Delicious, quick and easy! My kind of meal!

Of course, this year's variation for me will look like this: A slice of bread made from rice flour, gluten-free and vegan, toasted for a long time, because this bread is extremely dense; then spread some vegan mayonnaise, slice of ham (uncured), ring of pineapple (otherwise it's NOT Hawaiian!!), and topped with a slice of cheese. Here, I am planning on cheating for the sake of taste over health, because it's Christmas Eve, and I will &@#$#!@% have my Hawaiian toast!

Also, pineapple only had one evil red star on my forbidden list, so it's okay to have it every now and then. So, all in all, I'd still consider this within limits for the once in two and a half months' slip-up.

I'm planning on it, anyway. We'll see if I can pull it off, or if I'll feel too guilty having the cheese.

And again — Note to self: Erase the last few paragraphs before showing Doc my notes!

Day 76 – *Feeling of the Day*: Forgiving

Quick coffee with Victoria this morning turned into tea time. After my cold, I'm still dealing with cough and a bit of congestion, so tea was the perfect choice. She bakes some awesome Christmas cookies, so cheating my diet could not be helped. Had to have just one of her French cookies, and boy, it was good.

I also had one of my completely permissible gluten-free and vegan cookies. That was okay but definitely not the same as hers, but okay.

In any case, it's Christmas season, slip-ups to be expected – although I try to be disciplined. At least, that's what I would be telling my clients in my life coaching practice (helping people simplify their lives). "Don't be too hard on yourself if it's already done. Just fix the things you have control over (meaning future items entering my stomach!)"

Now, a quick permissible dinner before taking my boys and husband to see the latest movie in the Star Wars Saga!! Yay, Christmas time!!

Day 80 – *Feeling of the Day*: Responsible for my own actions

There has been a serious assault on my diet! Christmas Eve is the most special day of the whole year for me. We celebrate German style, opening presents on Christmas Eve after church. And it's the day I was going to make my exception to the meals with the Hawaii toast as described above.

However, the extent of the assault consisted of non-organic tofu for lunch, a slice of Christmas Stollen (traditional German Christmas cake), two slices of Kraft cheese (for two toasts in the evening), one piece of milk chocolate and another piece of chocolate and hazelnut!

I will probably have to make up for this by at least one extra week of the no-fun food diet.

Merry Christmas!

This morning I woke up not feeling great, but not horrible. Definitely not great like the days before.

I realize it's up to me to make sure I live well. It's all my responsibility, and nobody can tell me what I need to do or what I shouldn't do if I'm not willing to be disciplined by myself. I'm not cheating Doc or anybody else. The only person I am cheating is me!

So, the lesson learned today is 'I'm responsible for my actions in all areas, including my own health through food intake.' Yikes! But isn't that the definition of being a grown-up? I've already told my boys now, too, that they are responsible for their own health. I can only give pointers ("Eat your vegetables!"), but they are the ones who hold their fork and guide it to their mouth.

Day 82 – *Feeling of the Day*: Exhausted

And the assault continues...

It was 'traveling day' today, as we went up the local mountains to go skiing. Before we left the house, Rob made lunch, and it should have been a good one: Fried rice and kimchee in coconut oil. I was all for it until I saw him adding butter to the rice!

"I can't have butter!" I exclaimed, and he lost it! He was already stressed out from packing and getting the car ready for departure. On top of that, we ended up leaving a lot later than I had planned (in my head), and now this 'Butter assault'!

Hubby did not want to cook for his picky eater fam any longer!!

I felt bad, so I ate some after all. Aaron called me 'savage' for eating the buttery rice.

After our drive up, we went to pick up the ski lift tickets, checked into the hotel, and finally rented our ski and snowboard equipment. All that made for a very late dinner. The boys wanted pizza, so we went to the only pizza joint in town where I ordered the only meal on the menu that would work for me (my new go-to when eating out) – bunless burger with fries.

This is getting old.

Back at the hotel, I added two pieces of milk chocolate to the dilemma. I was just so exhausted and therefore not making good choices, I guess.

Why do I not have the same self-control that I had two months ago? Where did it go?? Shucks! My belly pooch is coming back out. I'm not happy!

And then, when I felt really frustrated with all the not-good-for-me food, I sat on the couch with a bag of tortilla chips and read the rest of the Christmas mail I had brought with me.

There was a Christmas card from my friend Dena, and it included a poem that read:

"'Twas the week after Christmas, and all through the house
Nothing would fit me, not even a blouse.
The cookies I'd nibble, the eggnog I'd taste
At the holiday parties had gone to my waist!"

And so on! I instantly dropped the chip I was about to eat and resigned for the night.

Skiing tomorrow. Hopefully that'll make me feel better!

Day 83 – *Feeling of the Day*: Undisciplined

Half and half creamer in my coffee from the machine with a major burnt taste. More chips at night. I'm not doing so hot! ☹

I gotta find that discipline again! I know I had it here somewhere!

Day 84 – *Feeling of the Day*: Probably gassy

So, I wonder, what happens with the specific type of food I'll be eating this week. All we have is the microwave in the room for dinner preparation, so I purchased lots of soups to feed myself: lentil, split pea, bean, etc. I know those types of food tend to produce some unwanted gas.

Not that a lady would be caught letting go of that gas, but I'm just wondering about the technical aspect of the procedure in my current situation. If I am on the slopes, packed into my ski suit, covered with the ski jacket, all closed up to the head, all zippers closed and buttons snapped shut, and then, should any of said gas escape accidentally, where is it going to go??

Will it stay in the hermetically closed internal space of my clothing? Or will it eventually find a way to get out and pollute the otherwise perfectly clean mountain air?

Hmm... things I never knew I'd think about.

Day 85 – *Feeling of the Day*: Optimistic

Finally, a good day yesterday and decent one today. No cheating on my diet. I even had salad with my dinner last night and a proper lentil veggie soup. One cookie after dinner and a piece of dark chocolate, but I still felt okay.

Today, I had that split pea soup, and we went to a fine Mexican restaurant for dinner (very soon after my late lunch, so I'm rather full now). An extravagant fish plate with veggies and rice that was so plentiful; it'll be my dinner again tomorrow! But all good within my rules!

For a relaxing evening in front of the TV with my boys, I had coffee with soy creamer and my own decent cookies. Although all within the rules and regulations of my diet, it was just a bit much today.

But then, I'm not worried too much about the quantity; I'll be back skiing tomorrow. ☺

Speaking of which, no broken bones, but I hit my tailbone several times. Once by the ski lift seat when I was ready to take a seat, but not properly aligned and the seat came swinging at me with all its might.

Then I fell on my behind once, right on that same bone, and one more time when I went to sit on the floor with my boys and I rolled backwards, again, right on the tailbone. Tailbone is not happy at all; it still hurts! Might have to get that checked when we are back from our trip.

Other than that, it's all good in snow paradise up here, and having a blast! I am very proud of both my boys who are doing so well snowboarding for only the second time in their lives and hubby is teaching me some skiing techniques.

Nevertheless, it's almost New Year's, and I already have my New Year's resolutions lined up. Back to no cheating the diet, do my neck and spine exercises (because I also have a problem with posture, I hunch over a lot and then get really bad backaches between my shoulder blades), and back to yoga as soon as the New Year starts!!

Yes, it's time to take charge again!

Will reinforce the resolutions tomorrow night, when we ring in the midnight fête!

Day 86 – *Feeling of the Day*: Fed up

This traveling to a very small town and staying for a week is proving to be rather challenging: There are several restaurants that do not serve any kind of food that's acceptable on my no-go list. Also, we are eating our lunches at the ski area in the car, tailgate style. So, every day I must bring something that I can eat standing up in the cold, and it must be enough to give me energy to ski.

I tried eating a peanut butter and jelly sandwich the first day, but the rice flour bread I brought is so dry, the dust is coming out of my ears. It really needs to be toasted. Twice! Then it's okay. I also had fruit, some snacks, until I noticed that conventional potato chips have caramel color (bad!) and yeast extract (bad for me!), so that took away my snacking fun.

Today, I had some leftover rice and a couple of slices of ham. Not so tasty when cold. I tossed the rest, so I'm out of luck for tomorrow. Looks like fries and a bunless burger is in my very near future!

Good thing I can have a decent dinner each night with my microwave soups!

All our snacks are in a basket, which we leave in the car. With the current temperatures, this is the biggest fridge we've ever owned! But there's been collateral damage! I brought (in good faith) several packages of soy sauce, and one must have gotten torn. There's spilled soy sauce in my basket and I am now down to 188 packages!

Day 87 – *Feeling of the Day*: Challenged

Happy New Year!

It's been a gorgeous day on the slopes with a brilliant blue sky, fresh glistening snow on the pine trees all around, and the view from the ski lift was incredible! We skied as much as we could in the morning hours, during which I worked on my technique to keep my skis parallel at all times. After a short (unsatisfying) lunch break at the car, we headed back for some more skiing when suddenly a cloud descended into the valley and made for very, very thick fog down by the ski lift loading areas.

We took the lift up to the highest slope and had the most beautiful view of mountain tops all around us and the cloud below. But then I realized that we had to get down exactly to where the cloud was hiding the safe haven of the resort area.

Starting out was fun, I got some speed (still very controlled, taking my time as a beginner), and got down to the last bit of the slope when I entered the cloud that was still sitting in the valley and didn't seem to move from there. I was on the white snow in very dense white fog! I've never seen so much white in my life!

I literally couldn't see anything but white. There was no way of telling where the snow ended and the fog began. It was only when I saw the shadows of the ski lift poles that I knew I was in the right area.

Another skier passed me, and I yelled, "I don't know where I'm going!"

"Downhill!!" was his answer. Made a lot of sense! I tried it and it worked.

I reached the bottom of the hill and went for a coffee break.

Puh, skiing is hard!!

Our last day of skiing is tomorrow and we'll be going home Tuesday back to the land of health food stores and an abundance of people who understand my (food) plight.

Day 89 – *Feeling of the Day*: **In denial**

Well, we're back home. I checked my weight this morning and it seems that I gained about 1.5 pounds over the last week. Must be some serious muscle mass I've developed through skiing!! I'm sure, all the late-night snacking and some of the cheating in my diet had nothing to do with this!

Day 90 – *Feeling of the Day*: Anxious with a side of headache

YESSSSS!!! Sushi lunch! We took out some of Rob's family to greet the New Year, and it was a perfect opportunity to get rid of THREE soy sauce packs! Down to 185 packs and just about done with three months of this experience, which means, it's almost time to get in touch with Doc and review my progress, and possibly, just possibly take me off the 'no wheat and gluten' restriction.

This one only had one evil red star out of three, and so it was not going to be as strict as the rest of them, but nevertheless, Doc felt that it would probably be a good idea to just go ahead and cleanse off those two items as well for three months.

I might, however, add a bit of time for all the cheating that happened over Christmas. Hmmm, is one week good enough? One month?!? Please, no! I'll have to ask him.

Meanwhile, it's been a headachy kind of day. I took half a pill this morning and was feeling blah all day. Not sure what caused it. ☹

Day 91 – *Feeling of the Day*: Good!

It's 5:43pm and I haven't cheated on my diet yet! It's a good day!

I stuck to all rules (protein breakfast consisted of cereal with my pea milk), lots of veggies for lunch (vegetable barley soup from Costco, very satisfying!) along with some roasted root vegetables, fresh fruit with my afternoon coffee (and a couple of small vegan and gluten-free cookies). There's only dinner left and I'm not sure yet what it'll be. But I'll try my best to be good for the rest of the day!

Also, it looks as though I am suffering from dystrophy. The muscle mass I gained last week disappeared after only a couple of days back home with good food, one day of cleaning out the garage and otherwise getting back into the home routine has done it. One pound gone!

Day 93 – *Feeling of the Day*: Challenged with my eating cycle

Let's talk about timing.

I had a couple of days with good, clean food, but my timing was off. For a variety of reasons, my dinner wasn't until 9pm for the last two days, and by the time the food was in front of me, I was so hungry that I ate more than I should have.

The food itself was good, but after the late-night meal, I couldn't go to sleep right away because I was feeling heavy. So, I stayed up until midnight, and that was still only three hours after my last meal. Two days ago, I got hungry again and snacked around 11pm. Again, clean food but not at the right time.

Consequently, I woke up the next morning feeling full. I had a small breakfast, ok lunch-size meal, but then not hungry in time for regular dinner, and therefore, a late dinner again. The downward spiral continues and would keep going if I didn't actively stop it. Today!

Thus, my lesson learned is, eat not only clean food, but eat it at decent times! If I'm not hungry, it's okay to eat a smaller portion, but eat in time before I get consumed by hunger and then overeat later!

Gotta really implement the following rules:

1. Eat the last bit of fresh fruits and vegetables at least six hours before sleeping.
2. Eat the last meal at least four (preferably up to six) hours before sleeping.
3. Maintain a period of 12-14 hours of no eating between dinner and the next morning's breakfast, so that my body will go through its own period of cleansing each day.

If I could truly follow these rules, I'd be super healthy! But these are hard, especially the last one. I can only try my best.

Day 94 – *Feeling of the day*: Really challenged

The last rule is REALLY hard to follow!

Day 95 – *Feeling of the Day*: Gums inflamed

Aaaah, first day of school, the boys are out of the house and I got to do my bookkeeping all day! I've been catching up from before the break and finished off entering all transactions for the past year. Tax season: Here I come!

Meanwhile, I've been having another episode of that gum inflammation. It's been a few days now. This one is very mild; I mainly feel the pain only when I floss, not even when I brush. So, it's still happening, but very, very mild in comparison to what I experienced before the no-food diet. I'm curious to see if it will stay this way.

10:57pm: Dang, that last timing rule is soooo hard to follow! Last bite to eat was at around 8:45pm (tomorrow's breakfast will be at 8am).

Day 98 – *Feeling of the Day*: Not great

Feeling blah. That gum inflammation spread to the other side of my mouth. It's still very mild compared to the intolerable pain while brushing that I experienced last year each time when that recurring inflammation hit. It is almost gone today, and I hope that eventually it will not come back ever.

Also, it was another somewhat headachy day yesterday, a little bit, maybe headache-ish. My head just wasn't sure if it should hurt or not, so I got away without a pain pill, but with a 45-minute rest in the afternoon and lots of water. I wasn't feeling all that great throughout the whole day.

Today I'm fine. I resolved to add three weeks to my diet due to 'Cheatsmas.' This will move my monthiversary date from the 6th to the 27th of each month. Should be a decent move (in my amateur mind).

Do I dare call Doc and ask about chelation to rid myself of those heavy metals that I have in my body? That was, in fact, the original reason I had contacted him for, when he happened to find all this other stuff. Now, I wonder if there's chelation in my near future as well. He had done the heavy metal test and found that there's a serious amount of lead and other bad metals in my body, but he thought it more important to address all those allergies first. Is now a good time for heavy metals??

Day 100 – *Feeling of the Day*: Hit by revelation

I found a strong correlation between my late-night eating, hours of sleep, and my belly fat!!

What a revelation! When I eat a bit late (even clean food) and sleep less than seven hours, my belly is still there the next morning and I am not a happy camper. When I eat earlier and get a good night sleep of seven hours or more (preferably more!), than my system digests longer and better, and my belly is much smaller the next day! It's like a game of 'Now you see me – now you don't!', only less attractive!

So, in addition to the quality of food and timing of my meals, the hours of sleep matter as well. For example, my body feels differently if I sleep six hours versus eight, even if I don't eat for twelve hours overnight in both cases, which should be a good cleansing period for my system. So much common sense, it almost hurts!

Meanwhile, the gum inflammation has moved to the upper left-hand corner of my mouth, more sensitive here, even when brushing my teeth. Not cool!

Day 102 – *Feeling of the Day*: Contemplating my cooking skills (or the lack thereof)

Gum inflammation is gone, thank goodness! I just hope it won't keep coming back. Yet another thing to heal if this food restriction should work!

Somehow, I've been waiting for me to turn into a miraculous chef preparing gluten-free and near-vegan meals that are tasty and shock the world around me to the core. From being a non-cook to becoming a specialist in this area, how does one do it?

So far at least, it's not happening. Maybe I need to cook instead of buying prepared foods from the health food store. Yeah, that might just do the trick!

For example, when I buy one of my favorites, the curry tofu salad at my local store, I might just have to look at the ingredients and try to mix it myself. Might end up being a lot cheaper, too. I should also try tuna salad. I've kind of been craving that, and I now know that I can substitute with Vegenaise (mayo without eggs and other evil ingredients).

Okay, ramp up that courage and dive back into the kitchen experiments! Oh No! It will be raining tomorrow through the rest of the weekend. When it's raining, Californians hardly drive unless it's absolutely necessary. Is it necessary to buy ingredients? Tomorrow??

I shall see how bad the rain will be.

Day 104 – *Feeling of the Day*: Anxious

This afternoon I contacted Doc to see if he will review the wheat and gluten restriction within my diet and possibly lift that ban. Both had only one evil red star, but his recommendation was to cut these out for at least three months so that I would not have any triggers for a while.

I'm waiting to hear back from him, fingers crossed, although, that is one of the least cumbersome restrictions. The markets are full of products that are gluten-free, so it's not as difficult. I so wish he could review my dairy issue, but that had three evil red stars, the highest rating, so the future is looking grim in the dairy world.

And yes, I did go buy some ingredients to make fish with rice and cauliflower tonight. I know, nothing new or super inventive, but I just had to give my boys a solid meal after a few random food nights. I also bought that curry tofu salad and am determined to write down the ingredients, so that I could try making it myself.

Was this one of my New Year's resolutions? I don't remember, but I think it'll be a good effort!

Day 105 – *Feeling of the Day*: Pretty satisfied

Yes, dinner was good last night. Even Aaron complimented me on the fish (which I only pan-fried with coconut oil, seasoned with basil). He turned the rice into spicy fried rice, adding coconut oil and Kimchee. A good cook for being only 13 years old!

Nobody but Rob and I touched the cauliflower; I was fine with that – more for me! I steamed it, added some salt, and filled my plate to the brim. I was really full after dinner, more than I had been in a long time.

Good thing, I know how to solve that problem: A double shot of espresso to ease my belly! Worked like a charm, only, I couldn't go to sleep until midnight. But hey, that's how I get my reading done!

Surprisingly, the fullness factor subsided not too long after dinner, and low and behold, when I stepped onto the scale this morning, I found that I am back down to the pre-Cheatsmas weight. I didn't weigh myself at the very beginning of this experiment (when I really should have), but going by what I think was my average, I've now lost a solid seven pounds and seem to be stable at that. I'm short, only 5'4" (and a half!), so seven pounds makes a difference: New pants for me!! ☺

Day 108 – *Feeling of the Day*: Happy

Yeah, baby! I'm back on the cooking train, making a solid dinner for the second time this week. This one is something I've never tried before. It's baked mini-meatloaves with baked apples, and I'm adding baked potatoes since I'm going with the baking theme tonight. The recipe calls for bread crumbs, but I substituted those for pulverized rice crackers. I used less than the recipe calls for, but added hamburger seasoning, so we'll see!

Aaron is already complaining that I don't alert him to the surprise dinner attacks in which he has to eat a combination of meat, potatoes, and possibly apples. He is looking for comfort food.

I've been thinking about why it is so hard for me to get on with the cooking. I like the idea of it and others can do it, so why can't I? I know, I'm not so creative in the kitchen, but I can follow directions. That means, I should not have a problem following recipes, and as it turns out, I've had some successes with those (I think... can't really remember now, but I'd like to think not all of them were failures.)

Maybe, I must come to terms with the fact that I won't become that superstar chef out of necessity, building my own brand of health food at the end of this experiment.

Maybe, I'll just become the best health food shopper, finding out which foods are decent and which ones are less exciting. Yes, I could become the number one gluten-free – somewhat vegan – elimination diet food taster!

Oh, dinner will be ready in five minutes. I'm curious to see how the fam will react!

After dinner: Not bad! Lucas gobbled up two and a half of the meatloaves (slightly bigger than a hamburger) AND packed the leftover for school lunch tomorrow! The baked potatoes were good, but nobody really liked the apples, or rather the rosemary on the apples. So, it seems there are no fans in the baked fruit department. I did like them after I slightly scraped off the rosemary. But everybody ate the meat, including Aaron! Clean finish!

It was only afterwards that I told Aaron about the one zucchini that was chopped and mixed into the meat. And he lives to tell the story!

Day 109 – *Feeling of the Day*: Heavy

Back to the weight issue – I'm back up by about a pound, and the only reason I can tell is because we now have a digital scale. Rob bought it, just because it was cheap. No other reason!

I think I vented about this before, so now it's full on IN MY FACE! We used to have a scale that took a while to adjust to your weight, swinging left and right, and then coming to a standstill, as long as you stood still. Those were the days you could squint your eyes and be convinced that the number you were seeing was high only because the scale was:

1. Never very accurate,

2. Your eyes were still tired because you just fell out of bed, and

3. The scale was moody and seemed to cooperate only on certain days anyway!

Now, no such luck! It's digital with large numbers in black on light blue. There is no mistake in the number!

Regardless, one pound is nothing to fret over. However, I've not been getting my minimum seven hours of sleep per night over the last week, and my belly is back out.

Hmmmm, coincidence?!?!?

I can tell if it is a good day or not by looking at my underwear while wearing it:

Good day: It sits on top of my belly and I can see the front when I look down! ☺

Bad day: It sits under my belly pooch and I don't see the front of it when I look. ☹

Today, I can't see a thing down there! I need more sleep!

Day 110 – *Feeling of the Day*: Caught in a reality check

Just to clarify: The days when I can actually see the underwear in the front when I look straight down are rare! Always have been.

Since the beginning of the no-food/no-fun-diet though, those days had increased, simply because my body had gone through all these changes and shedding some junk, so I thought this is how it's gonna be! But with time, the regular shape reappeared and although lighter, my belly issue has remained.

Day 111 – *Feeling of the Day*: Excited

I'm very excited!! I have an appointment with Doc for this coming Monday to discuss the wheat-gluten restriction. He called, pulled up my chart on his computer and then remembered, "Oh, I'm blinded by all the red stars on your chart!!"

Just as a refresher: Red stars on the allergy panel are those that say:

* Sensitive: Eat only once or twice a week

** Allergic: Do not eat for a year

*** Evil: Do not be in the same room with me, do not call or write, do not ever think about me again!!

Wheat and gluten only had one star each, but, as a precaution and to jump-start my healing process, Doc had recommended that I cut both of these as well in order to avoid any of the feather-ruffling within my gut. Not that I have feathers there. . . that I know of anyways!

Day 112 – *Feeling of the Day*: Suffering the consequences from bad eating

Girl's night out last night! It was a lot of fun, but I slept poorly, and my stomach was hurting during the night. Now here are the potential culprits:

- Kung Pao beef for dinner (wondering if there was any MSG involved?)
- Two mugs of coffee in the early afternoon at home, then a cappuccino in the late afternoon and an espresso after dinner
- Anxiety over a business strategy that I discussed with my two friends

Hmmm, which one is responsible? Not sure. I'll just do better today.

However, as a general rule, I find it more and more doable to go to a restaurant and pick a complete dish that fulfills all of Doc's wishes! ☺

Day 113 – *Feeling of the Day*: Unhappy with a slight headache

Argh, headache today! The day started with just the smallest nagging pain in the back of my head, which slowly grew to warrant half a pain pill in the early afternoon and me having to go to bed.

Now, I really have no idea what could have caused this one.

Day 115 – *Feeling of the Day*: Unhappy with a strong headache

Headache AGAIN! No fun, but today may have been caused by the change in altitude. We went back up the mountain for another day of skiing. Naturally, to pull this off during a regular weekend took some planning and preparation, a very early morning drive of 1 ½ hours and then getting all the equipment rented and still being on the slopes by 8:45am so that we could use the day completely.

Not to mention, we were taking eight people total, our family and friends! So today we were responsible for another three middle schoolers and our good friend Tanya (she's all grown-up and quite responsible herself, so not much supervision necessary. ☺

It was the most brilliant day; crisp blue skies, fresh white powdery snow dotted with some green pine trees. But it was very windy and still cold, and that, I think, was the start of today's headache.

I took another half pill, snacked a bit, and finally, finally on the drive home, I was able to close my eyes a bit. I'm okay now, but really, really tired!

Hoping for a great visit with Doc tomorrow! Good night!

Day 117 – *Feeling of the Day*: Miserable with a stomachache

It's a new month with new rules! I saw Doc on Monday and as it so happened, we weren't just discussing the State of the Union, but also doing the first chelation IV. The IV is filled with an agent that will trigger the heavy metals to leave my bones and tissues that they've settled in and be gone!

I'd had the results from the first lab test proving that, indeed, I did have lead and mercury in my body; in fact, significantly more than desirable! Now it is a matter of testing how much would come out in a provoked test.

Boy, that was miserable!! Not so much the IV; that was actually a relaxing experience because I got to sit on Doc's La-Z-Boy sofa seat with my book and did not have much else to do. We discussed all the things I had questions on, such as:

- Is it ok to drink lots of water with the meal?
  - o Doc: "No, because the water dilutes the acid in the stomach just when it is necessary to be at pH 2 to digest the food. Drink outside of your meals, like around 30 minutes before or after is fine."
- Alkaline water. Yes or no?
  - o Doc: "Not with the meal for sure (see above), otherwise may not be necessary, but some of my patients tell me that they do feel better with it."
- How often can I eat soy per week?
  - o Doc: "As with all the foods, you need to rotate as much as possible. Eat any type of food only 2-3 times a week. That would be ideal!"
- How can I escape rice (think rice, rice milk, rice bread, rice crackers etc.)?
  - o Doc: "See above, just pay attention to what you eat today and don't eat it tomorrow, if possible."

That was all good information!

I do have a habit of drinking lots of water with my meals; this will be the biggest change I have to make out of this. That along with not having cereal with pea milk every morning.

I'm a very routine-liking kind of girl, so I do get stuck that way easily. Now I must find two or three more things I can eat in the morning. Problem is the only bread I have found so far is made of brown rice flour, so that means I'm already eating rice that day. The days I have the rice bread in the morning should then also be the day with rice for lunch or dinner. Lots of rice on those days, oh well.

Oh man, this is hard. Balancing on a beam is easy for me. Balancing LIFE??? Oh dear!

But back to the misery of chelation (which is the bigger misery): I finished the treatment just fine and went home to drink the second of three powder drinks I must drink the day of and the day after the IV.

That drink will help absorb the chelation agent along with the metal it found, and then go to my filter (kidney) and eliminate (pee)! Well, the drink isn't all that tasty, but then, none of the medical drinks really are.

Well, the last one in the evening hurt my stomach. I think I drank it too fast. I went to bed and woke up at 3am with a stomachache! No more sleep for me that night and the pain continued the whole next day!

I was basically slumping around in my bathrobe all day, hurting. Thank goodness, Rob was home yesterday and able to take Aaron for his doctor's appointment after school. I just stayed in and couldn't eat much at all.

I still had to drink my three drinks over the course of the day, as Doc confirmed after I sent him a text. Things seemed to get a little better in the afternoon, and yet, I was hardly able to finish the last drink. The stomachache came back in the evening. I went to bed with it, but I was able to sleep through the night. I woke up this morning, and . . . Nothing!

It's over! Hurray!! I already went for a walk this morning, greeting the world into which I have been reborn! The sun is shining, the birds are singing! It's that kind of feeling! ☺

Whooohoooo! Now we just wait for the lab results of the pee I had to collect the day of the IV. This will then tell us how bad the metal situation really is. And it will determine if the continuing treatment will be either done with more IVs, suppositories or oral treatment (eating pills). I'm crossing my fingers for the oral!

Very, very much!!!

Day 118 – *Feeling of the Day*: Evil

Muahahaha! I cooked pasta with Bolognese sauce tonight and the boys did not discover the shredded carrots in it!

I also substituted the heavy cream with a mix of my soy and coconut creamers (only ¼ cup required anyway). Seemed to work!

Bwahahaha!! Feeling GOOD tonight!!

Day 119 – *Feeling of the Day*: Bored with my bread choices

I need new bread! This is really getting old....

Doc had given me a few websites with info on alternative breads for purchase online and another sheet with a list of gluten-free bakeries in the area. Well, the best site I looked at indeed had a few options viable for me, but one must order at least four breads in order for them to ship. In a flash, my total for a possible order was nearly $50! – For bread!!

Not great! So, I decided to look up 'Do it yourself' recipes. The hardest thing seemed to be the 'no yeast' rule! Gluten-free is quite easy now!!

I found several videos, which ranged from 'looks like even I could do this' to downright hysterical!! What are these people thinking?!?! That ain't easy!!!

I picked two recipes that I wrote down. One for flat bread, which I would toast in a pan and one for a loaf of bread baked in the oven. I am excited to try these tomorrow!

Day 120 – *Feeling of the Day*: **Somewhat accomplished**

I went to buy all my bread ingredients this morning. The first recipe called out for a mix of buckwheat, rice and corn flour. I really want to avoid both, rice and corn, since I'll be running into the same issue of too much rice and also too much corn (cornflakes, corn chips, corn pasta…). This bread is supposed to give me a break from both, so I looked at the supermarket shelf to see what exciting options there were for substitution.

I picked spelt flour and all-purpose baking flour (which comes in a gluten-free variety). I had just found a website that stated that rye flour (which I still had at home) actually contained gluten, so my fabulous Christmas cookies for which I had used some rye flour, turns out, weren't that fabulous after all!

Well, I didn't use that much of it, and they tasted good, but all in all, I should have avoided it, had I known then…

Back at home, I googled spelt (my phone did not get the Internet connection right there at the store unfortunately), and so it was only then that I found that spelt also contains gluten! Go figure!

Maybe, I should just do all the research before I go into such an endeavor?

After lunch, I was ready in the kitchen to go to town with all my shiny new baking supplies! I whipped up the first batter for the loaf of bread, wildly substituting my flours to make a buckwheat, spelt and all-purpose mix.

The lady in the YouTube video was right. This was a very easy recipe and the dough was almost cake-like. I was able to fill my baking dish very easily. It did not require any kneading. Once I had this one in the oven, I went ahead to mix the second batch for some flat bread.

Even less ingredients of only flour, water and salt.

It was extremely easy to mix, but then required kneading for 5-10 minutes. It was a lot stickier than I expected, so I kept adding flour to get it to a decent texture for making a ball. Then it was time to make smaller balls of the dough, roll them out and toast them in the pan for a few minutes each side until it started to develop little air pockets.

There was no oil required for the pan. This worried me a little because I wonder if this could ruin my pan. The recipe had said to use a pan with a heavy bottom. I don't have one of those. I am using a hard-anodized aluminum pan.

More so, I got bored after a while with the making of dough balls, flattening them into small circles, and then toasting them one by one. Originally, the recipe called for nine balls to be formed, but I guess, I made smaller balls and ended up having fourteen. It took a long time to work on all of these because each one had to be toasted on both sides individually.

Meanwhile, the other bread finished baking (one hour!) while I was still toasting the flat breads. But in the end, I had everyone in my family taste a piece of flat bread and they all survived and found it generally edible.

As with the bread loaf, maybe more salt next time. It is a little bland, but hey! I baked bread!!

Day 121 – *Feeling of the Day*: Looking forward to a fun day

Super Bowl Sunday!! We are invited at a big party and there will be tons of food!!! I am sure, I'll find something to eat, and it's after lunch anyway, so I can just look forward to a relaxing, fun day with friends and our whole family!

Late evening: Oh, My Goodness!!!! That game was way too exciting and a challenge at the same time! Our family was divided over which team we were rooting for, but in the end, we are not hardcore fans anyway. We just love the company and fun!

Food ended up being a challenge! There were two large buffets: One with hot food and one for desserts. Sooo much good food; it was a feast for the eyes! The things I could eat (and did plenty of) were corn chips with salsa, corn chips with guacamole and a fruit salad.

I also had two espressos, which resulted in miserable sleep last night (I didn't realize it was already late when I had them).

For dinner, I had more corn chips. Hubby ended up drinking a beer and a Schnapps (which he usually doesn't), so he was drunk and needed some real food before we went home. He had more ribs and all kinds of good stuff that I couldn't have. So, I had more corn chips.

Back home, I made a hot lemon tea with honey for Aaron who is coughing and has a stuffy nose. I had one, too, and felt really full. Not pleasant. Full of corn chips – the unsalted kind.

On the upside, Doc had told me that I should do my wheat experiment this weekend, but I have yet to pick a day. I need one where I am 100% in control of my food. I want the aftermath of Super Bowl corn chips to go by without affecting my findings of wheat consumption. I picked this coming Thursday to be my 'Big Day of Wheat'!

I am looking forward to it!!

Day 122 – *Feeling of the Day*: Logical

I've lived in the U.S. for about 21 years now, most of this time in Southern California. You would think that I should know how to make my own guacamole by now. We're having our book club meeting tomorrow night, and it'll be a Taco Tuesday theme, so I was thinking about contributing the guac.

But the best recipe I know for guacamole is to open the tub from the local health food store! It's delicious with a creamy texture and I, myself, have never attempted to make it because why mess with something good?

Yup, I'll be bringing my flat breads, vegan and slightly gluten-free (except for ½ cup, divided by 14, of spelt flour per bread), as an alternative for the flour tortillas. Heck, I've eaten more corn chips during these past four months than I probably have over the past four years!

Three days until my 'Big Day of Wheat'! I definitely should plan this week's menu carefully.

Day 123 – *Feeling of the Day*: Crushed

Ok, now I feel like crying. I sent an email to Doc asking about the oat-, spelt-, and rye- gluten situation. I wrote that I truly had not known that these contain gluten, but I had consumed some of it during these past three months.

"Was this a problem?" I asked.

Doc said, "Yes!"

Gee, how should I have known??? I am new! Oats contain gluten? WHY???!!?? And who put it there?!?!?

Does this mean I wasted these first three months and must add another three with a truly gluten-free diet? What else contains gluten? How would I know all these details?!? I'm not a dietician! Do I need to hire one now who is well-versed in the naturopathic ways?!?

My only consolation is that my German language-tutoring student will come to my house any moment now, and learning German grammar is probably still harder than trying to find out where all the gluten is hiding!

At least, I'll be sitting with someone for the next hour whose misery is truly more difficult to bear. I'll have a distraction!

Day 124 – *Feeling of the Day*: Discouraged

I am so frustrated! I spent an hour this morning at the store, trying to find more breakfast alternatives to my cornflakes and rice bread. Something, obviously gluten-free, but also free of yeast. It seems that anything remotely bread-like is either made of rice flour or corn, or both.

I don't know how to get more variety into my food! I am trying to avoid overloads of rice, corn and soy to avert future problems, but it seems almost impossible.

In a world where buckwheat is not wheat but rhubarb, peanut is not a nut but a legume, coconut is not a nut but fruit, how am I supposed to find my way around?!?!?!!!!

I AM SO FRUSTRATED!!

I want my life back! I want pasta! I want chicken!!

I don't even know if I should have my 'Big Day of Wheat' anymore. Might have to send Doc another email, but that may not end well.

Late afternoon:

Fiiiiiiinnneee! I'll bake again, second trial. I will only do the bread loaf since I have no need for flat bread at this time and the loaf was super easy to make. The hardest thing about that is grating an apple. I can do it!

Day 125 – *Feeling of the Day*: Seriously depressed

Noooooooooooooooooooooooooooooooooooooooooooooooooooooooooooo
ooooooooooooooooooooooooooooooooooooooooooooooooooooooooooooo
ooooooooooooooooooooooooooooooooooooooooooooooooooooooooooooo
ooooooooooooooooooooooo!!!!

I must start my gluten-free time over!!! No 'Big Day of Wheat' for me!

I had, ever so tentatively, texted Doc with my question, "Given my ignorance of gluten products and past inflictions on the restriction, should I still have one day of wheat this week to test for any reaction?"

Doc responds, "Since you were consuming gluten, it would not prove anything. Need to be free from gluten for a minimum of 4 months, longer is better." This is where I choked up.

He also suggested I read "Gluten-free for Dummies." Yup, just what I needed!

Day 126 – *Feeling of the Day*: Sad

Just as I got Doc's message about having to do it all over, Lucas was sitting at the table and saw me getting sad. He asked if I wanted to come and sit right next to him. I did.

Then he held me and said he was sorry I could not eat any of the good food. That was comforting.

Day 128 – *Feeling of the Day*: Miserable

Bad news and more bad news! The whole family is down with a nasty cold (thankfully not the flu!) and it's a long weekend. I am miserable and it's the second time this winter! Why?!??

Even worse, I got the results from the heavy metal test. Not good at all! My lead and mercury levels are literally off the chart! Aluminum, nickel and uranium are also "outside reference", and four other metals (including arsenic!!) are outside of the 'green' area. The detailed report states 'exceeds expected level' for these. But for lead, it states: "This individual's urine lead exceeds three times the upper expected limit per the reference population." SERIOUSLY!!

Remember how miserable I was after the chelation IV and drinking a total of six powder drinks for a couple of days? And how I was crossing my fingers to get away with oral chelation (think: supplements)??

Well, it's not happening! Nope!! I am going to have to go through with all IV treatments if I want to get this out of me within 12 weeks. It'll be a weekly procedure for the next three months, starting tomorrow!

Alternately, I could go with suppositories, but that would mean shooting stuff up my behind for at least a year in order to remove all that junk.

Speaking of junk, I wonder if I could get money for all that metal. After all, some of it is precious.

?!??

Sooo, not only do I have a diagnosis that's depressing, I also have the most expensive treatment ahead of me. Unpleasant, too, although Doc said, after three to four IVs, it should start to hurt less. That's encouraging!

Well, why am I not surprised?!?! But the more important question is:

HOW THE HECK AM I STILL ALIVE?!?!?!?!??!!

Day 129 – *Feeling of the Day*: A little bit relieved

Yup, it's a day of IV, driving to Doc's office, which is about 15 miles from my house. That itself is not fun. Normally, 15 miles would not be much at all, but it's 15 miles over the 405 freeway, which has been dubbed SoCal's biggest parking lot.

And since there's no school today, I must take Lucas with me (Aaron is shadowing Rob at work today for a school project), so Lucas is not amused either. This is just great!

Okay, okay. I gotta keep it in perspective! My father-in-law must go to dialysis three times a week. I should not be complaining at all! Ok, I stop.

Late evening:

Well, it all went better than expected. Lucas ended up staying with our sweet neighbor Emily and her four-year old boy. They played for the entire time I was gone!

Doc had to search for my vein and ended up sticking me a few times, but that is not new to me; happens all the time. I might look like a drug addict when I'm finished after the last IV (ten more times).

Doc also answered all of today's questions. For example:

- Is coconut milk ok? Yes, it's not dairy, but still only use coconut at a maximum of about twice a week. Also, I learned that most oils are not pure, so even organic coconut oil will most likely still contain some of the proteins that I should not have every day. It very much depends on the quality of the oil.
- Cocoa butter? Yes, because it has no dairy in it (I thought so, but after being found out as the gluten-free dummy, I thought, I better check everything now).
- Dill seeds? They are okay because they are not seeds! (go figure!)
- Flaxseed meal: No!! ("Bad patient, bad!!")
- Take all vitamins, etc. together with my breakfast tea? Yes, okay because everything else would stress me out even more.

- Will my bones become porous after chelation, when all those metals are drawn out? Ha! Doc could not answer but found it to be an interesting question. I suggested he write a thesis about it after some research.

After this surprisingly pleasant visit, I breezed through less traffic than expected. When I came home, Rob and Aaron had just gotten home as well, so we decided to be total rebels and skip soccer practice in favor of going to the movies!!

I've also managed to drink all three powder drinks so far and just a tiny bit of stomach twinge, but really, not bad at all. Feeling pretty good about that . . . so far.

Day 130 – *Feeling of the Day*: Optimistic

Well, it seems that this last IV treatment was not so bad after all! I finished both days of powder drinks and they went well with very minor stomachache. This is how I did it: I really took my time drinking each drink, probably between 20 – 30 minutes each!

This morning, I even managed to go on a walk with my friend Kate. She walks with two boxer dogs, so it wasn't as slow as I might have taken it by myself. But, of course, I don't want to appear like a wimp, so I bravely marched on.

Things are looking up! Only 10 more weeks, 10 more IVs to go.

Day 132 – *Feeling of the Day*: Energized

I've been thinking about the "Gluten-free for Dummies" book. I feel that it might be a waste of money, just because I only need it for four months. But then, since I am a dummy in this department, I should probably buy it anyway.

I went to the bookstore today to take a look at the book. I found that it not only contains lots of information about the pros and cons of gluten and gluten-free foods, but also some pretty easy recipes. That, in turn, inspired me to look at some gluten-free books for baking, simply because I like baking better than cooking. I found a book that is altogether gluten- and dairy-free, with little symbols showing what else it omits for each recipe (e.g. nuts or eggs or yeast etc.). This seemed handy for me, especially after browsing through the health food store for over an hour earlier today and finding, yet again, that my diet is just too expensive to buy ready-made stuff.

Motivated myself by making the bookstore richer! Yay!!

Day 134 – *Feeling of the Day*: Joyful

There's no way I can mess up tonight's dinner! It's going to be Mongolian Beef, in the crock pot, only six ingredients:

3 lbs. of Beef (fajita meat)
½ cup of soy sauce,
2/3 cups of brown sugar,
½ cup of water,
4 cloves of garlic and
½ tsp of ginger.

Only six, I can't get this one wrong!

I am cutting the beef into cubes, measured the soy sauce, water and sugar just right, chopped the garlic and minced the ginger, it'll be fine. Right?

Well, it's all in the pot, stewing. The recipe says seven to eight hours, so it'll be done between 6 and 7pm. ...should be good ☺

With rice and some roasted broccolini...

After dinner:

I did it!! Everybody liked it, each and everyone in the family!!! I am so happy!! Finally, a dish that Aaron immediately complimented (except that the meat was almost too tender and practically falling off the fork), and Hubby had no time to comment, he said, because he was too busy eating fast!

Puh, finally! This dish received four stars (one full star per family member), and Aaron even asked if I could make this once a month or so. That's a good measure, I am peaceful tonight.

And there are leftovers for tomorrow! The best!

Life is good after all!!!

Day 135 – *Feeling of the Day*: Snacky

I am saving the Mongolian Beef leftovers one more day, so that I won't be eating the same thing several days in a row. Paranoia, do I hear thee?

Tonight's dinner consisted of gluten-free pasta and tomato sauce with lots of mushrooms. No protein, just leftovers. ☹

Even though I ate throughout the day, I felt quite hungry during dinner. I served myself seconds and then snacked on tortilla chips afterwards, and then finished off with a couple of pieces of dark chocolate.

I haven't snacked like that in a long time. Because I have been eating so well and quite disciplined for the last four months, I don't feel bad about tonight. I just can't make it a habit again!

Better go brush my teeth now before another snack attack hits!

Day 136 – *Feeling of the Day*: Chugging along

The third IV today: It went quite well and had a friendly chat with Doc while sitting in the Lazy Boy again. Our conversation was completely gluten-free! We talked about raising children (ah, the good old days), the cost of living in California (prohibitive), and giving birth in Timor where Doc worked in a clinic for about six months several years ago (astonishing)!

I am feeling okay with the IV, just a little queasy in my tummy after finishing that third powder drink tonight. Three more drinks tomorrow and nine more IVs hereafter. That makes 54 more powder drinks for those nine IVs, plus the three tomorrow: 57 more powder drinks! Yuck!

Oh no, that prospect is just way too depressing. I better just go back to doing my IV countdown and be a happy camper with that.

Meanwhile for dinner, I had some of the tuna salad I made a few days ago. I was very excited about how well it turned out because it was my first attempt ever! Lucas looked at it curiously and I gave him a small bite to try.

Shouldn't have done that! He liked it so much that he finished it off! Now I've got make more.

Day 137 – *Feeling of the Day*: **Full of good ideas**

I'm a genius!! I'm a genius! Imma genius!!! On my way home from the store this morning, I was dreading the upcoming powder drink, when suddenly it dawned on me that I could mix the orange flavored powder into some orange juice instead of water!!

What a concept! Doc had noted on the prescription to mix the powder into a non-carbonated drink, but since I usually don't drink juice, it was the most mundane thing to mix the powder into my water.

But NO! Not this time!

I came home and saw that we had some orange juice left, which hubby had bought not too long ago. I mixed and yes!!!! It is delightful if only slightly sandy (the powder does not all dissolve).

Now, the new downside is that I'll be drinking six glasses of juice over the course of two days! I still must drink it slowly or else (stomachaches)! But it's a much better prospect than 57 nauseating drinks coming my way. Hey, only 56 now!!

Afternoon:

Out of orange juice; but acai juice works too! Just tested it with the powder and it's all tasty and good! ☺

Down to 55 drinks, one more tonight and then we're back on next week! Now, the whole chelation IV thing should be a piece of cake! As long as Doc finds my veins! Can I call "Find my- i-vein"?

Day 138 – *Feeling of the Day*: Intimidated

I am highly intimidated by the amount of root vegetables I bought this morning. I had some roasted root vegetables the other day from the market (already prepared), and I know that this is the kind of veggies I should have more of. I also remembered that I had seen a recipe in a magazine that I tore out and saved because it looked doable. So, I figured that I could give it a try!

I listed all the veggies on my shopping list (some of which I truly didn't know what they looked like. "What's parsnip, anyways?") and went on a shopping spree.

Hey, I might not be a cook, and am a dummy when it comes to gluten, but not knowing what parsnip is, is not all my fault! Don't forget, I'm not only kitchen-challenged, but I'm also an ESL student. English is not my first language, and if there's any German language student out there, not a cook (!), who could tell me what 'Braunkohl' is, then we'll talk!

But back to my veggies. I've bought a pile of things, which I'm looking forward to getting to know. I'll be cutting these up as necessary (following the pretty picture in the recipe) and roasting in my oven to make a large batch so that I can feast on it for several days.

Crossing my fingers!

Day 139 – *Feeling of the Day*: Surprised at my findings

I am getting more sensitive! Since Doc told me last week to not have water with my meal, I've been following his advice and have felt fine not having my drink. But today, Rob and I went out to lunch and, purely out of habit, I had the full glass of water along with my food. Afterwards, I could tell that my stomach felt heavier for a longer time. Now it made total sense! The water dilutes the stomach acid and, therefore, the stomach has a harder time digesting the food!

Crazy to think that I've done it all my adult life, but after such a short time of abstaining, I can feel the difference!

Or maybe, I'm crazy and it's all in my head?!?

I'm also very excited about a new find! I have discovered red lentil pasta! I'm curious to see how it compares to the black bean pasta that I had tried quite a while back. On a 'hit-or-miss' scale, that black bean pasta was definitely leaning heavily towards the 'miss' section, according to my personal taste. So, I will try the red lentil pasta; just not sure yet when it will fit into my dinner plan (because I only made half a dinner plan for this week and it ends after tonight.)

We're having friends stay with us over this coming weekend with their two little kids, so all bets are off as far as dinner is concerned for the larger group. I might always just take care of my boys and then myself separately, or have the guys hack out a plan to feed the masses. They're better at barbequing and making up stuff quickly.

Day 140 – *Feeling of the Day*: Half-way excited

Aha! The gluten-free and dairy-free baking book arrived today, and I read it in one night! Mainly because it has so many pretty pictures! I'll still have to do some substituting because of my egg restriction, but all in all, I hope I can get some good use out of it!

I can't seem to muster the same enthusiasm to read my "Gluten-Free for Dummies" book. Well, one day. One would think that I should really read this book first, especially if I want to avoid prolonging my diet to infinity and beyond!

Day 142 – *Feeling of the Day*: Exhausted

Puh! Just finishing off a super busy weekend with house guests and another skiing trip. But I am proud of Lucas who made another batch of tuna salad based on the recipe I had found. He tasted it and found it agreeable! This was the on-the-go lunch for me at the ski resort and will be my lunch again spread out over the next few days!

And no, I will not eat it two days in a row!

Day 143 – *Feeling of the Day*: Must abide by logic

I can't believe it's already time for another IV today. I am getting ready by having my fabulous powder drink mixed in acai juice and water. This is going to be just fine.

On another note, I will be asking Doc some more questions today, and I am afraid of one of them:

"Do I have to cut out all the foods that are processed in a facility or on equipment that is shared with 'evil' foods? Sometimes, I've found statements on the packaging that'll indicate that the food "may contain traces of …xyz…" Is this going to be a no-no?"

Maybe, I should really be reading the "Gluten-free for Dummies" book! I guess, simply owning it does not make me smarter in this area. ☹

Late afternoon:

Sure enough, Doc's answer according to my expectation. The purer I eat, the better the chances of healing the food allergies. In other words, if I can avoid foods that are processed on shared equipment with wheat or dairy or other forbidden foods, then I will be that much more successful in actually making it through this year and really having made a difference.

As a 'normal' person, if I eat 95% pure, then I will be 95% better. However, this does not apply to Celiac patients. They must follow a much stricter regimen. But even in my case, I should aim for the purest possible foods.

Hmmm, not great, but it makes sense.

Day 144 – *Feeling of the Day*: Like a rapper (only in white-girl version)

Aha! Here is the solution to my question about constipation. Not such a pleasant subject, I know, but it's a thing and I have felt a little more constipated since eating more rice and dark chocolate than I had before.

My go-to solution used to be yogurt and flaxseed, both of which I can no longer have. But Doc told me yesterday that a concentrated dosage of vitamin C, somewhere between 4-6 grams in one intake, will do the trick if you really, really need help! About two grams will be absorbed by the body and the remainder will sit in the intestines, draw lots of water from the body into the intestines, and the rest is pure chemistry.

So, without seeds and dairy, vitamin C is the key to good chemistry with the toilet!

Ooh, this sounds like a rap!! Let me try, here we go:

Vitamin C
Is the key
To having good chemistry
With the toilet.

If you're constipated
And you hate it
Try vitamin C
And spoil it. (the constipation)

How about that!?!?!?!!! Hah!

Day 145 – *Feeling of the Day*: Heavy

Oh dear, I am so full after dinner; it's not funny!

And I was good today, following my new-found eating routine:

Breakfast, including a protein, mid-morning snack of roasted and salted beans; lunch, which included my tuna salad in a gluten-free wrap and stir-fried veggies, followed by coffee with a shredded coconut cookie and one piece of dark chocolate; fruit in the afternoon and then disaster struck.

I had to go clothes shopping with Aaron and Lucas, and we ended up coming home just around 7pm. We got to eat dinner around 7:30pm, which is too late, and after dinner (root veggies, potatoes, more stir-fried veggies and a little piece of ham for protein), Rob brought out my apple pie.

I say 'my' apple pie, because it is one that I found at a gluten-free and vegan bakery. Tanya had told me about the bakery and since it is not too far from Doc's office, I decided on Monday that I should go check it out.

They had a variety of cupcakes, some bread, one small apple pie, cookies, and other goodies. Out of all the gluten-free and vegan baked goods, I could exactly have one thing – the apple pie.

Everything else had either nuts or seeds or something else that disagrees with me. The apple pie was only ten dollars, so I snatched it up! I was determined to treat myself!

It was small, and if I ate one quarter as a serving, I think, I would have been satisfied. Well, I didn't stop at one quarter, more like about half tonight.

Why can't I stop in time?!?!?!!

In all fairness, half of the pie is gone, and Rob did help me with it. However, once he found some milk chocolate that I can't have, he decided that I should have the pie and he would sacrifice himself eating the foods I would leave alone.

By the time I finished my dessert pigging out session, it was about 8:30pm. I now need to stay awake until 2:30am for my last meal to finish six hours before bedtime.

It's 11:40pm and I give up! I'm tired, going to bed! This is not going over well with my tummy!

Tomorrow morning, I have a coffee date with Victoria, and I'll have to eat really skinny stuff so that I can feel better. Yup, that's gonna happen!!

Day 146 – *Feeling of the Day*: Recovering

It didn't happen – the skinny stuff, I mean. We had coffee alright, and for snack we usually have fruit and maybe one little cookie or piece of dark chocolate. Not this time! No fresh fruit, so we made do with the rest of the goodies.

I woke up with a heavy stomach, no surprise here, since half the apple pie was probably sitting in there. Eventually, the feeling of heaviness subsided, and the rest of the day went by with decent food choices. Now, there's only dinner left, and I will make SURE that the apple pie has no reappearance tonight.

Not for a good while, anyhow!

Dinner will be pasta casserole for the family (one of the boy's favorite dishes) and a split pea soup for me (from the package). Good enough for tonight.

Day 148 – *Feeling of the Day*: Getting organized, then hungry

I have started to write down what I eat throughout the day in order to keep track of the foods I consume. Rotating food is the new mantra to keeping a good (food) balance. I was beginning to get so stressed out. It's incredibly difficult to remember if I had soy or peanuts the day before or not and to think about which of the breakfast foods I had eaten in the last two days and what I needed to rotate. All of that turned this whole experience into a very nerve-racking event, introducing a very new type of stress that I never knew before!

I even make check marks for the number of glasses of water I consumed throughout the day because I was worried about not drinking enough (which is soooo important.) Especially now that I don't drink water with my meals anymore, I have to remember to drink in between. (Oh, that reminds me – I should go get a glass of water while I write this.) And so, I found myself stressing over all of these food issues way too much!

I also find it a lot easier to write down the foods I ate after the fact rather than making a dinner plan. Hmm, I wonder why?

It's time I get back to making real dinner plans. My eating has been clean, but not stellar. It's a real challenge to feel full and satisfied when I don't have enough food for me at home. Especially protein sources! I am trying to eat protein with each meal, but I haven't prepared much recently, so I am scrambling to find food.

Yesterday I ate a decent breakfast, small lunch with some protein and lots of veggies, tons of fruit in the afternoon and (out of circumstantial necessity), In-N-Out Burger (protein style, no sauce) for dinner while on the go with the family. Now, that should have been filling, but it wasn't!

I sat on the couch later, when I really should have gone to sleep. But I just felt like watching a TV show, so I did. While I was sitting there, don't you know it, I got hungry! Not just a bit snacky! No, I was hungry!

So, I am breaking out the salted and roasted chickpeas (protein) and snacked on those. But then I remembered that I had gotten a tummy ache from these before when I overdid it. I went and got tortilla chips instead and ate some of those, but of course, that's not ideal. So, I go and get Veggie Straws. Those are light and puffy! ☺

I rotated those three alright (in the spirit of rotating foods!) and was finally able to put an end to it when the show was just about over. I'm a grown woman and I still manage to make some dumb choices. It's quite fascinating! Who ever thought of putting me in charge of raising two boys?!?

This morning, I feel surprisingly fine. Not as bad as I was anticipating after a night's snack binge like that. It's probably the veggie straws with their puffy lightness.

I might eat a few more and get lift off!

Day 149 – *Feeling of the Day*: On a Shopping High

I went to the health food store today in order to fill the void in my fridge – even before making a dinner plan for this coming week. But that's ok. I had finished all the roasted root vegetables (very tasty!), so I bought some new ones today to restock as a side dish readily available. I even remembered the parsnips! I also bought a whole cauliflower, a package of edamame and some Marsala sauce. Apparently, I'll be doing some cooking this week.

Then, I wandered around the store, looking at all the packaged foods in the freezer section to see if there was anything I could eat. There was more than I expected! I bought one of every package that works for me. I now have a fantastic mix of gluten-free battered halibut, kale puffs, lentil and garbanzo bean medley, and lamb vindaloo in my freezer. This will be interesting.

I wonder if I can hurt my taste buds. Can they get sick?

Day 150 – *Feeling of the Day*: Grateful

Chelation IV number five today! Suddenly, time is flying by! To have a weekly marker makes it easier to see how I am progressing, rather than trying to remember the month. That reminds me today marks a big day – The FIVE-month anniversary of my new diet!! Woohoo!

Still on the uphill timewise but looking good!

I am also having lunch with Tanya after my IV today. She works nearby Doc's office and there are many Japanese restaurants in the area, so chances are I might have a sushi lunch today. It's been forever!!

In the evening:

No sushi lunch today; we went to a very cute Mediterranean café instead that just looked perfect for lunch while sitting outside in the warm sun. I had a spinach salad (without pecans or feta), and a side of vegan potato salad. Interesting combo, but I am no longer surprised at my own food choices.

However, for dinner, I had the red lentil pasta, the one I bought a little while ago and it was actually quite good ☺ and a very good source of protein! This one passed! I had tomato sauce with it; I think that made it tasty.

The IV went well also, although my left arm was not cooperating in producing an agreeable vein. It seems that I have hit another high of cleansing action with the chelation, too, because during today's IV (and the one from last week), I can feel something rushing through my body. It's the weirdest sensation! A little mix of feeling dizzy and unreal, just as if I had been awake for 30 hours.

On my way home, I stopped to get some more groceries (since yesterday's shopping at my regular health food store was as so successful, I thought, I could do even better at the other one a few miles away today!) Well, I needed some of my pea milk, which apparently no other store carries.

I am very fortunate to live within a four-mile radius of four different health food stores. It makes it so much easier to go through this experience and even make fun of it for my own good. Yes, I am very fortunate!

Every time I complain, just think of me as a whiny brat with some first world problems!

Day 151 – *Feeling of the Day*: Evaluating

Time to take stock of my health. After all, it's been five months that I have followed my new diet plan and I should reflect on what has changed.

For one, at some point yesterday, I thought, I was already six months into it, so apparently gluten-free food makes you lose your math skills!

Other than that, let me see . . . hmmm, what is different?

Well, here we go:

- I lost seven pounds within the first two months and regained two, but I've been at this weight steady now
- My finger joints do not hurt any longer, no pain at all, which is huge, because that was a daily pain. It wasn't major or debilitating, but annoying. Now, it's gone.
- In the area of hair loss, I'm not sure yet, because the hairiest episodes of loss have always occurred during summer, so I'll have to wait and see. For now, I'd say that the amount of hair loss in the shower has been fairly normal
- Definitely less headaches. I used to get them a few times a month, maybe two or so, and bad enough to take me out for the rest of the day.
  The last few headaches I had may have had distinct triggers, such as altitude or extreme temperature changes, but then, it's difficult to pinpoint headaches anyway. They may or may not be triggered by certain foods. I have not found the one and only true culprit, but in any case, it's been less and that almost makes me want to cry with relief!
  From what I can see, the last headaches I had were on January 27th and 29th and beginning of December before that. This is HUGE!!!
  In fact, the temperature rose by over 11 degrees from yesterday to today, and no headache, not even the slightest twinge anywhere in sight! This used to be a migraine-provoking circumstance for sure! But not today or any of these last few instances!

- The last gum inflammation happened about two months ago. It's been quiet on the gum front ever since, hoping this will continue, too!
- My skin seems to be getting better. I am breaking out less, even though that has been a constant since I was 16 years old (at least!).
- No more feeling bloated after a big meal!

On the down side:

- More stress over counting how much water I drink throughout the day, monitoring the food variety and obsessing over rotating the foods; also stressing over cooking for the family, now with the added level of difficulty, especially since cooking doesn't come easy for me.
- More constipation; might be from increased rice consumption, although I have tried to keep it at a minimum. Could also be from all the vitamin supplements or more dark chocolate.

If that is it on the down side, I think, I'll be ok!

Day 154 – *Feeling of the Day*: Finding my stride

Still finishing off all the packaged meals I found at both food stores last week. They've all been tasty if maybe a little small in portion. I am adding vegetables, pan-fried (which is almost the only way I know how to prepare eggplant, bell pepper and zucchini), and it makes for a decent meal.

Following all of that with fresh fruit, and I am full enough!

Today, however, Friday is a day to go out and eat at the local health food store with Hubby, so my freezer will stay closed (and still quite full), and my kitchen clean!

It's a good day for my diet! ☺

Day 157 – *Feeling of the Day*: Stuck

I am officially having a bad vein day! Today is the day my vein formally ended its amicable relationship with Doc. "It's not you, it's me!" it said, as it turned around and rolled away each time he tried to stick it for today's IV.

Last week he had tried my left arm in a couple of spots (I still have that bruise), and finally went into the right arm. Today, he tried the right arm, the right hand in two different spots, my left forearm, and about 30 frustrating minutes later, I walked out of the office – No IV!

It's not Doc's fault. It's always been difficult to have blood drawn because my veins shrink the moment they see a needle. It's a challenge almost every time. I've been stuck up to six times in one visit (not at Doc's office, but elsewhere), and so far, it had been going surprisingly well here. Up until today.

Doc offered to have me come back 1 ½ hours later when a phlebotomist was going to come in to help another patient get an IV started. Apparently, that poor person has really bad veins! This phlebotomist could help with mine as well, since that is what she does all day long – Stick people for money!

I had no idea such a profession existed! I didn't even know how to spell it until I tried a few things on Google (with varying results).

1 ½ hours later: She is good!! She got my vein and hooked me up to the IV on her first try! "I love you," I whispered. I don't think she heard me. IV number six, halfway through! ☺

She will be coming back each week from now on.

Day 158 – *Feeling of the Day*: Stomachache

Still waking up with stomachaches. The powder drink has improved vastly through mixing it into juice, but it's still grainy and makes me not want to drink it. I don't feel so good.

On the upside, I have a book club meeting again tonight. That makes my day all better.

Day 159 – *Feeling of the Day*: Okay

Last night was Book club. We intended to go for a walk since it was only a very small group. We met at Starbucks until all the members appeared (only four of us) and started our talk. I left two hours later without a walk (unless you count the distance from the car to the chair inside Starbucks).

Nevertheless, I'm feeling decent today since I worked out at the gym (which is rather unusual). I don't like the gym and it does not like me. I can't stand the smell. When I leave, I smell, too. It must be the gym's fault.

I noticed, though, that my tummy is sticking out again, rather unpleasantly. This could be from an overdose of food or lack of sleep. It's been a row of nights with just around six hours of sleep, and I didn't even get to binge watch anything! The boys' schools and other things in life have just been busy. Like that's a surprise!

In order to simplify the next couple of dinners, I bought roast chicken for the boys, and excellent grass-fed beef for another go at the Mongolian Beef, which had been so well-received.

I am loving my preparedness!

Day 160 – *Feeling of the Day*: Ingenious

I was told by Aaron and Lucas that the roast chicken was dry. How could that be? I bought it during lunchtime, and then stuck it in the oven to heat it up again while also baking French fries. Does that take the moisture out? Hmmm, note to self – next time, buy the chicken only when you want to eat it, like right that minute!

Today, I prepared the Mongolian beef. It was fun to gather the few ingredients, until I noticed that my bottle of gluten-free soy sauce was almost empty. I contemplated a quick run to the store, when suddenly I remembered, "No! Wait!! I have soy sauce!!! In tiny little packages!!!!"

It took fourteen little packages that I had to open, in order to fill the remainder of the half cup required for my fantastic Mongolian beef. Now, I lost count of how many packs I have left because I don't remember when I used them last. I might have to sit down and make soy sauce piles to count the remainder, just for the fun of it.

Dinner in about one hour. I can't wait to see if it'll be as tasty as the first time. I have a feeling that I might have put a little more ginger than what the recipe calls for.

1½ hours later:

The meat was great if not even a little too tender. It practically fell apart when trying to stick it with the fork. Aaron's friend ate with us and everybody seemed to like it. Again! Now, I better give it a rest for a while before everybody gets tired of it!

This was a good cooking day! I am happy!! ☺

Day 161 – *Feeling of the Day*: Soy-happy

178 packs of soy sauce left! I counted!!

My kitchen looked a little odd with piles of soy sauce packs, piles of ten each in neat rows of five, and then the odd row with two piles and eight individual packs left. But it was very organized and orderly. As we say in German, "There must be order!" ;)

I am glad to know that I have my number back. I was kind of curious anyway to see if there were really 200 packs in the box when it arrived, and not, you know, maybe only 194. Because who would sit down and count the packs upon receipt?!?!?!! That would have been soy fraud, but nobody would ever know because nobody would ever really count!

Well, I am glad to know now that I have not been soy defrauded.

Last weekend I found out that someone had stolen my credit card info and tried to defraud me there, so I had to close that account, but at least, no soy fraud in this house! That's something!!

Day 162 – *Feeling of the Day*: Full of dermatology questions

As I mentioned before, I think, my skin has gotten better with my new nutrition plan. It's been clearer and smoother. But I also bought one of those miracle moisturizers, that is supposed to transform your skin within minutes, and "It's yours if you buy it now and pay shipping and handling fees only for the introductory package!" It was a total impulse buy, I admit, but it was advertised so cleverly. I figured what the heck, I'll try it.

I was almost surprised that the moisturizer was delivered to my house. I thought it would be a total scam but then I started using it, and it seemed to really help my skin! I totally believe that it already has reduced my wrinkles!

Unfortunately, one thing that has not changed through diet or other means is the fact that my eyes are starting to go bad. It's advancing age; there's no way around it.

Last year, my eye doctor prescribed glasses for me, and dutifully, I bought them and then put them on my shelf. They didn't help at all!

Today, however, I noticed that I was really straining my eyes when sitting at the computer, so I got the glasses off the shelf, put them on, and shockingly, the screen and everything further away suddenly seemed sharp and clear!

I also caught eye of myself when I turned to the side and saw my reflection in the closet mirror doors. All my wrinkles are back!!

Either the moisturizer totally failed me today or glasses are bad for your skin!

I haven't decided yet which it is. I must investigate further!

Day 163 – *Feeling of the Day*: Disappointed

I am so sad. My 1½ month streak of no headaches has come to a screeching halt today.☹ We are in the middle of a 'superbloom' after several years of drought in California and then a very wet winter. So, naturally, I must go see!

I drove about two hours out of the LA basin, over the mountains towards an area that has several lakes and found a hike along a hilly area that had tons of wildflowers. It was really beautiful! I did not, however, anticipate that this hike would be:

- Going up a steep small mountain to overlook the lake in a valley
- Be in full sun exposure
- Be six miles long (round-trip)
- Be taking place from 10:30am–1:30pm (with snack break, extensive photographic sessions, etc.) when the temperature rose to 91 degrees Fahrenheit.

I carried water, of course, and my snacks. I kept checking that I had enough water left to last until I reached the car (where I had more water). And all the way up and down, I felt good, constantly checking inwardly if I felt a headache coming on.

Until I reached my car again, I did not. I was so proud because I thought, "Yes! I am getting stronger, and I am not getting headaches anymore!!!"

But no! A headache started when I sat in my overheated car, drove back to town (which took about 30 minutes) in order to find a place for lunch, and then finally ate lunch around 2:30pm.

I really wanted some Mexican food. I had some yesterday for lunch with friends, and it was so good. I figured I could eat some more today. So, I finally found this little place, but it was not that great and surprisingly not air-conditioned. I think I won't be eating a bean tostada for a very long time now. Even the guacamole looked like paste that had been squeezed out of a tube. I couldn't even . . . no, I couldn't!

I had plenty of corn chips, though, they were good. I ended up eating too much so that I also started getting a little nauseous on the way out. I stopped for coffee before heading home, but it did not make the headache go away. That is when I decided that I needed to take half a pill after all. Going home over the mountain didn't help the nausea. At least, I was driving (which I had to, since I was by myself!).

I'm really bummed. But it was a pretty good painkiller-free run, while it lasted. Starting all over tomorrow for, hopefully, an even longer time without headaches.

Day 164 – *Feeling of the Day*: As strong as Popeye

Another IV day; it was the funniest so far. The phlebotomist's name is Twinkle. Seriously, how uplifting is that! She tried to get into my left arm vein after checking both arms and checking again. It didn't look so good. She tried anyway because the two previous IVs both went into my right arm. Better to change it up a bit so that I won't be mistaken later for some junkie.

In any case, Twinkle had me make a fist around one of those rubber squeeze balls and pump my hand so that I'd get the vein popping. Then she said to just hold the hand still and she went into my arm with the needle. I almost didn't feel that one at all, but she couldn't get into the vein. It kept rolling away. After several inner-arm poking attempts, she said that it was no good; this one won't work. She told me to relax my hand, but I couldn't! She pulled out the needle and removed the rubber strap that was supposed to slow my blood flow. But I couldn't open my hand! I had squeezed the living daylights out of that ball, so that my fingers were now stuck to it, and I couldn't get them off.

She had to pry my fingers off in order to remove the ball out of my hand. It took a moment until I got the feeling back into my fingers. Unfortunately, the ball is dead! I'm afraid I now owe Doc one of those.

Twinkle laughed all the way home, but not until after she went into the right arm, got the vein on the first try, and walked away!

Day 166 – *Feeling of the Day*: Irritated

I am experiencing a rotational impasse.

On Monday, I had food that included potato, corn, rice, and quinoa. Mainly from the gluten-free pasta that I made for dinner, which includes corn, rice and quinoa. That's a load of the foods I could be rotating.

Tuesday, I had buckwheat in my breakfast bread, soy in the format of tofu for lunch as well as in my creamer, and the same pasta for lunch. I figured that it was within the same 24-hour period and is Doc-approved. That made for more corn, quinoa and rice on the same day. I also had stir-fry veggies, prepared in coconut oil.

Now, quinoa and coconut both had one evil star (out of three on my list), so I should not have these more than twice a week.

Today, I had a rice and buckwheat waffle in the morning, so I was going to eat a rice-dish for lunch, but when I opened the fridge, I saw the leftovers, and this is what happened in my head.

Simple and practical thinking (from before the no-food diet) lead to an automatic reaction thinking, "Well, I could just finish the leftovers." So, I ate the pasta, again!! Didn't even think twice about it!! But that now constitutes the third day in a row I had corn, rice and quinoa.

With my afternoon coffee, I had coconut creamer, which I shouldn't have because I already had coconut yesterday. But then I also had the tofu yesterday, so I should not have had soy creamer today.

Aaaaaaarrrrrghhhhhhh! This is getting so complicated! It's making me crazy! See what it's like to be inside a perfectionist's head!!!!!

I realize that having the pre-made foods like gluten-free pasta or bread made from all-purpose flour or waffles and other things from a package are really not helping because they mix all of the foods that I should eat on alternate days.

So now, I really, really need to avoid all those allergens that I had over the last three days, but that means, I really can't eat anything at all tomorrow! Hmmm. Tricky!!

Day 167 – *Feeling of the Day*: More resilient

I feel very good today! Weirdly enough, it's because of a near-headache experience. Today was very busy, lots of running around in order to prepare a casual baby shower for Emily this Saturday and then an all-out birthday party for Aaron who is turning 14 on Sunday!

It also got hot suddenly, and I felt the twinge in the back of my head coming on. Possibly slightly dehydrated, too. By the time I got home, wondering whether I should give in and take one of those pain pills (or half to start out with), I tried with one small homeopathic pill, two mugs of coffee and lots of water, and the headache went away!

I am so happy! I really think my body is getting more resistant! If I can just curb those headaches alone, I'd be very, very happy for a long time!!!

Day 168 – *Feeling of the Day*: Blah

OH MY GOSH, that was bland!!

I had decided to stay away from all those allergens I maxed out in the beginning of the week. I needed to skip the previous three breakfast choices that I'd been rotating diligently in favor of, ta-da, oatmeal! I never eat oatmeal because it just doesn't look appealing to me. But since I needed to find something different for today, this was the only thing that came to mind.

I have gluten-free oats which I filled into my bowl and then poured hot water over it, just as I've observed hubby doing it. I added dried fruit and fresh banana slices which quickly turned into the highlight of the meal. The longer I ate, the less exciting it got.

There's an expression in German that you eat something you don't like 'with long teeth' to avoid touching it with your tongue or gums, etc. I ate my oatmeal with very long teeth. Finally, since the banana pieces were the best part, I abandoned the oatmeal and simply ate the rest of the banana separately.

I guess that was the health-food version of having a cupcake and just licking off the icing.

After finishing, I realized that there's several things I could have done to the oatmeal to make it tastier. Maybe add some cinnamon (which I'm not sure if I even have any) or honey or even my newly beloved xylitol, but I forgot.

With the xylitol, I'm just afraid that one day I won't have it available, but then, I might be totally addicted to this new sweetness that I'm now adding to my coffee and other things! So that's not a good thing either.

Two more mornings this week to fill with better breakfast ideas. Hmmmm.

Day 172 – *Feeling of the Day*: Recovering from too much fun

Oh my, I made it through those breakfasts with another round of just fruit and a roasted chickpea snack later for protein. Okay, starting a new week with refreshed diet solutions (maybe). It was a crazy weekend with the baby shower on Saturday and throwing an all-out birthday party for my now 14-year old Aaron on Sunday (from 9:30am till 7pm!!).

To top it off, hubby and I went with friends to be in the live audience of *Dancing with the Stars* yesterday, so that was three consecutive days of nearly more fun than one can stand!! The show was great, and we went for a fabulous (modified) dinner afterwards. Now, I might need to go through a cleanse, ha!

In order to have something sweet available for myself to celebrate all those happy occasions this past weekend, I baked a vegan, gluten-free banana chocolate cake. I found the recipe online and it was pretty simple.

The result was not bad. It needs to be a little sweeter. I think that could easily be helped if either the bananas were riper, or if I added more sweetener (the recipe calls for agave syrup, but I'm sure my new friend xylitol would work as well).

I should have had another IV yesterday, but I preferred DWTS, since I had the opportunity. Will go for IV tomorrow because that's the next time Twinkle is available, and I won't go anywhere without her from now on (as far as going into my veins is concerned)!

Day 173 – *Feeling of the Day*: Tense

While waiting in line at DWTS to be seated inside (this alone took about 3½ hours), hubby asked me if I was excited. And that's when I noticed that instead of looking forward to the show, I was fretting over not having enough water (which we weren't allowed to bring inside) and therefore getting a headache. Also, I had to make sure to keep eating, so that lack of solid food would not result in a headache either.

Why was I so focused on trying to avoid a headache when it wasn't there? I should have been excited about this opportunity!! I know I don't do well when I don't drink enough or don't eat in time, but maybe I just fret too much, thereby creating the headache I am worried about getting later!

What a concept! I am possibly stressing myself into a headache over the fact that I might get a headache!!!

Stop it already!! I need to relax a bit more, loosen up, come on, what am I? 90??

I did smuggle in a small bottle of water, and had some roasted beans in a baggy deep down in my purse, so it lasted just enough, and the headache never came – at least not full on, just a slight pressure that went away as soon as we sat down in the restaurant after the show. The show was great; very interesting to see how differently the TV version comes across!

Day 174 – *Feeling of the Day*: Getting comfortable

Today is hubby's and my 21st wedding anniversary. Must celebrate with a nice dinner out. I'm not sure yet where we'll go, we'll see.

Yesterday I had another IV. Twinkle stuck me three times to get into a vein. ☹ She says this is called 'rolling veins'. I've heard of rolling hills or roly-polies, but rolling veins? Maybe my veins are really just friendly and polite! "Oh, look! A needle coming in here. Let's move over and make space!"

For dinner, I made a potato and pinto bean chili recipe that I found in a magazine. It was nobody's favorite, so guess who gets to eat all the leftovers!?!

Well, at least I am starting to get a little more adventurous when I see recipes. Last night's recipe called for just one kind of bean, onions, potatoes, veggie broth and seasoning. But I wanted to make it a little more filling, so I fried onion with ground pork in the pan, added chopped green bell pepper, salt and pepper and added all that into the pot with the beans, potatoes and broth. It made for a much thicker stew, seasoned according to the recipe.

I thought it was not that bad at all (now that I had my second serving for lunch today). I am proud to report that even Aaron ate two bowls of it last night. He had complained of an overload of rice and meat dinners recently, so this was a nice change.

Meanwhile, I am also getting into a nice routine of soy, coconut and pea milk rotation with a three-day turnaround of these. I should be okay with my creamers for coffee.

Only six months into it, and already, I feel comfortable with my creamer rotation routine.

Day 175 – *Feeling of the Day*: Fulfilled by an elegant dinner

Last night's dinner was nearly fabulous! We ended up going to a French Crêperie, beautifully decorated with heavy red velvet curtains around painted windows, luxurious extra-large mirrors framed in ornate gold hanging off the walls and chandeliers sparkling down from the ceiling. I ordered a Crêpe Ratatouille, which is a crêpe filled with tomatoes, eggplant and a few other vegetables all mixed and stewed together. I asked, however, to drop the crêpe, so I actually had a plate full of vegetables, ratatouille-style. No cheese on top.

To make up for the lack of substance, I ordered a side of garlic fries. Delicious!

My boys and hubby each had beautiful crêpes, filled with a variety of mouth-watering bits, and topped it off with a dessert crêpe filled with Nutella!

It. Looked. Really. Yummy. The longer I looked at it, the yummier it got!

I was steadfast and ordered a soy cappuccino. Since the garlic fries had a very strong aftertaste, I really had a garlic cappuccino. I think that is indeed unconstitutional and should be prosecuted!

Day 178 – *Feeling of the Day*: Exhausted!

Today is a new week, a new IV! Where did my week go? Oh, yes, I remember! It all started Friday, a week ago with a dinner party with friends; Saturday: Baby shower; Sunday: Birthday party; Monday: Dancing with the Stars; Tuesday: Tango night; Wednesday: A big, black, empty hole; Thursday: Wedding anniversary; Friday – Sunday: Rob out of town; Monday (today): Overnight guests; Tomorrow: Tango night; Day after tomorrow: Dead on the floor, exhausted, mayyyyyyybe watching some TV.

Well, it's only been five days since the last IV, so, of course, this time it seems like an extremely fast turnaround! This will be IV number 9! I can't believe things are moving so fast now. Only three more after this! The only thing I am not looking forward to is peeing in the bucket after IV number twelve, in order to collect specimen over the course of six hours. A sample of that must be sent to the lab to determine how much heavy metal remains in my body. Hopefully very little!! Crossing my fingers and toes now!

This past weekend it just so happened that I had In-N-Out Burger twice. I know, that's not good. I know, I know! But it happened due to football and other schedules, so there it is! I did that. Always protein style (without the bun), replacing the spread with ketchup. Safe, but not great.

Nevertheless, I always follow my diet restrictions. I only had a small bite of Aaron's birthday brownie, that's it! I swear!! Just one crumb, really.

I am falling into a new food trap, though. I used to eat chocolate every day. It's embarrassing, but true! Every single day! After I started this new diet, of course, I could not have any milk chocolate. Because I ate so differently, I lost the habit of eating chocolate and I started to not miss it either!

I couldn't believe it, but I really did not miss it!

I do know, however, that I could have dark chocolate when there's no dairy in it (since cocoa butter is not butter ☺) and I have found a few brands of dark chocolates that I can eat. Now, I've started eating dark chocolate again every day just like I used to eat milk chocolate, and instead of eating just one small piece, I now eat at least two or three pieces. You see where this is going?

I eat it after my fruit with my afternoon coffee or as a small piece of sweet after dinner. It's not great, and dark chocolate does not satisfy the craving as much as milk chocolate did for me. Maybe I need to lose the habit again altogether, so that:

- Number One, I don't get addicted to chocolate again
- Number Two, I don't invite constipation into my life, and
- Number Three, avoid eating the same thing (especially sugar!) every day, which I know is bad, bad, bad!!

I need to coach myself to cut back and calm things down overall! Will do!! Ummmm, how about on Wednesday?!?!

Day 179 – *Feeling of the Day*: Being reasonable

I coached myself (one day earlier than I planned) and, as a result, decided to skip tango tonight. Bummer, but I've really been so tired over the past few days that it will be better for me in the long run to get to bed at a decent time for once (and not wait another day, dragging along without energy).

All in all, this should be an easy evening. I need to read a few more pages in my book for the book club meeting next Tuesday (which I will be hosting!). I picked Andre Agassi's autobiography *Open*, and it's excellent, emotional, and intense. I really feel good about myself as a parent after reading the first few chapters and learning about Agassi's father being such a tennis fanatic. On top of that, Agassi's wife, Steffi Graf, is from Germany (just like me) and that makes for a special connection (along with the other 80 some million Germans out there).

On another note: Yesterday, Twinkle got me on her first try after feeling and inspecting all my veins for a good long while! Doc said the vein she decided to go into would have been his third choice. Twinkle had already figured out that the other two weren't going to work that day. She said the vein they both had used several times before just didn't have enough bounce yesterday. Sticking fatigue.

Well, my veins are rolling and bouncing along in there? Who knew that veins have a secret Zumba life in my arms?!?!

Day 180 – *Feeling of the Day*: Messed up again!

Yesterday Rob cooked a delicious Korean meal with spicy BBQ pork to feed our overnight guests. The meat must be marinated in a hot pepper paste and is then fried in a pan along with onions. Very tasty!

We had rice with it. I filled my plate and even went for seconds. Afterwards, cleaning up the kitchen, I noticed the container with the hot pepper paste sitting on the counter. I picked it up and read the ingredients: Wheat!!!

OH NO!! I had a full plate of the meat with wheat!!! The horror!

Now what?

Lucas asked if this would add a week to my diet timeline to make up for it. I said I don't know, but I'll have to go make a confession at Doc's office next Monday when I'm going back for the next IV appointment.

Why is life so complicated? And why is there wheat everywhere???

Day 181 – *Feeling of the Day*: Marking a milestone

Today is a big day!! It's been six months since I started this no-food diet when the evil red stars on the food allergy list took over! I can't believe it! Really, six months!!

Suddenly, it doesn't feel as if it has been this long. As I promised myself, however, I'll be going on to the end of April to mark halftime due to my ever so slight cheating on my diet with improper food over the holidays and the spicy Korean BBQ wheat pork incident this week. So, I'll be doing the proper celebration of THE halftime event at a later date!

Last night I stayed up until 1 am reading Agassi's book. It is sooo good! But shouldn't I pursue an earlier bedtime so that I can re-establish a healthy routine with more regular sleep?

Oh balance, where art thou??

Day 183 – *Feeling of the Day*: Disappointed in myself

I had a great morning, meeting with two of my friends for an early morning walk and then breakfast. We met at a cute little area with souvenir shops, boutiques and many restaurants by the water. The only true breakfast place, however, is a very homey, traditional place. Breakfast here means all waffles, pancakes, omelets.

Hmmm, can't have any of those. I looked at the salads on the menu, but somehow, salad for breakfast is all wrong. Then I remembered that I can modify their creations which now opens a whole new menu for me: I order a smoked salmon omelet without eggs! The waiter looked at me as if I'm from a different planet. So did my friends! "You want an omelet without eggs?!?? So, what do you want?"

"Just all the other stuff that it comes with! The salmon, the capers, onions, and, oh, by the way, could I have some potatoes on the side?"

Now the waiter's face lit up and he suggested that I could have hash browns as a side! Perfect!!

I am glad to have options! This is actually not breakfast food in my book; it's probably a really early lunch, but it's okay. I have food!

Then, a good while later the food arrived and my smoked salmon, the capers and onions are covered with melted cheese…! Oh no, I feel terrible!!! Absolutely terrible because I forgot to tell the waiter to hold the cheese.

I told the waiter "I am so sorry, but I can't have the cheese!" He asked me if I wanted the no-egg omelet redone and I said yes, please, but I still felt horrible. I just hope they didn't throw this food away, but instead that someone of their staff got to eat it. Maybe

I am so disappointed in myself because I remember the very first time I had to have a full plate of delicious food returned to the kitchen due to my own mistake, forgetting to let the waiter know that there can't be cheese on it.

At that time, I watched the waiter take the plate back and trash the whole thing. I felt so, so bad! It had been my mistake and I told them I would pay for the second meal just like the first, but he wouldn't hear it. Oh no, it's part of customer service, but it felt so wrong to me!

That first time this happened, all of this food craze was still really new, so I was just learning to find a new way around restaurant food. But by now, I should have remembered! This incident should not have happened!

I tipped the waiter really well when paying for the meal. And I am still feeling bad about sending the dish back.

Later in the day, I made another cardinal mistake. Rob prepared dinner again tonight as we had friends over. We had rice and BBQ beef that was not marinated but seasoned. I kept asking Rob about what he used to prepare the beef, but he kept telling me that it was just a dry rub. I asked him: "Is this just pepper? What did you use?" He finally said that it was prepared at the grocery store. Now I am sure that this was a seasoning mix from a bottle which I also know now will almost certainly contain yeast extract.

By then, I ate a good two helpings of meat.

On Monday, I am facing Doc for IV number 10 and must do penance.

Day 184 – *Feeling of the Day*: Meh

I woke up and felt as if my fingers were slightly swollen. Was it the yeast extract that I am sure was in the dry rub? Or the fact that the meat was not organic, but good old mainstream hormone beef?

I don't know. Maybe both.

We went to the beach early morning with the boys for some surfing and boogie boarding. I walked in order to make up for a lot of sitting yesterday (in the car, at a long breakfast, back in the car, at home with our friends for coffee and dinner, then with another friend coming by to pick up her son). It turned into a day with very little movement, and I don't do well with that. I like to move around.

So, this morning, I used the time to walk a lot. Afterwards everybody rinsed off and we headed over to church followed by lunch. Everybody was tired from a long weekend with lots of company. I started to feel a little pressure on the back of my head, right-hand side. After lunch, I cleaned up briefly and then took a nap. Aaron came in three times to ask me questions, but still, I finally got to sleep a little. The headache started up just then, but I managed to fend it off with a lot of water and coffee!

No need for a pain pill. I am so glad!! This is becoming an almost sure thing; the fact that not every slight twinge will turn into a full-blown headache. Life is good this way! Puh, I can breathe!!

Nevertheless, I know I need to take it easy tonight and make my way to bed early enough. It's possible tonight because I finished Agassi's book. It's not taunting me, calling my name any more. I finished and am very satisfied with the ending! ☺

Day 185 – *Feeling of the Day*: Somewhat relieved, but not entirely

Ok, so I told Doc about my two missteps during the past week. He was glad to hear that I felt a difference because he said that is the golden standard – To be able to tell if something does not agree with my body.

I didn't really feel anything after the spicy marinated pork so wheat might not be the worst for me. But the dry-rub beef did something to me, so I'll know better next time.

He also said that I didn't have to add time to my current year in order to make up for these meals. Now that's good news! Finally!!

Then I brought up my other worry and that didn't go as well. I am traveling to Germany next month, spending about 12 days with my family. I'll be on the road quite a bit, and so I am worried about food options then. I know, health food stores are available, but they are usually not as big as here, which means much more limited choices. I'm not sure about what I'll find and what I'll be able to eat. Mostly breakfast, I think, will be a challenge. My dad likes to go to the bakery for breakfast and have some of the good, fresh rolls that come in all kinds of flour combinations, with seeds or without. I love the bread, but I am pretty sure, the entire bakery is a no-no zone for me right now. ☹

Doc said, 'Well, how about bacon and eggs? Can you have eggs?"

I said 'No!'

"Oh. Maybe just the bacon then?"

"Yeah, but not at the bakery. And I don't really like bacon that much"

I should have told him about eating an omelet without eggs last weekend.

Doc hastily left the room and that was the end of my food discussion for my upcoming trip. Hmmm.

Evening:

Tired and late for dinner, I made a really stupid choice for my meal. I ate bean chips and salsa with corn chips as a side and then leftover grapes — just so I can get the container washed because our fridge is too full (mainly full of stuff I can't have)!

Rob had taken the boys out for some errands and they ate on the go, so I was left alone for dinner. I wasn't hungry for the longest time; it was past 8pm and I still hadn't eaten anything, and then this all seemed like a reasonable snack. At least, at the time it did. Not so much now after I'm feeling a wee bit too full of non-vegetable food.

I guess, I keep thinking 'protein'. Must have protein!!

Day 186 – *Feeling of the Day*: Definitely not like a food wizard!

I committed another food sin today. I'm really doing this up, aren't I?!?!! It is the day of my book club meeting, and I am hosting today! I'm very excited about it, so I went to the store to view my options at the salad bar to provide at least something edible for myself and Olivia, who is also gluten-free.

There was a meatless chicken salad. I sampled a small cup of it and was only mildly impressed, but I thought, it'd be something new. I asked the lady behind the counter if it was made of tofu and she responded: "No, it's soy!" Oh, okay, glad we clarified that!

Then she proceeded to pack a small container for me and when she handed it to me, I read the label. The salad contained yeast extract! Of course, by this time, I had finished my sample which consisted of several spoonful of meatless chicken. Again, with the carelessness on my part!!

So instead, I bought Hawaiian slaw even though it contained poppy seeds (two evil red stars on my no-go list). I still had some for dinner anyway. I had also gone out to the vegan and gluten-free bakery near Doc's office to buy a mixed berry pie that is 100% permissible in my book, and boy, did that taste good!!

My personal book club dinner tonight: Hawaiian slaw, strawberries, watermelon and pie. Seemed like a good idea at the time. ☺

It was a very fun evening. Happy to report that everyone seemed to really like the book (Andre Agassi's autobiography) and our discussion was lively! I now want to go and meet Andre Agassi and his wife Stefanie, formerly known as Steffi Graf!

Afterwards, I had some pie left over, which had been my secret hope. I cut it into three pieces and froze them which I will thoroughly enjoy on Good Friday, Easter Sunday and another miscellaneous day respectively!

Day 187 – *Feeling of the Day*: Amused

Hubby came home from a day-long business trip with a co-worker and complained about the co-worker's driving skills.

He said: "Man, he can't drive!! It was terrible! At least, I'm a good driver, only, I fall asleep!"

"Well," I said, "That could be considered a flaw."

Day 188 – *Feeling of the Day*: Pitiful

And yet another unsatisfactory dinner tonight! Aaron had a flag football game tonight and it was late when it ended. All four of us were there: Aaron, Lucas, Rob and I, so we debated whether we should eat at home or go out to eat. Boys and I strongly advocated towards going out, but Rob wanted to go home. He tried to get the boys on his side by offering to cook Korean noodles (total junk food), the very spicy kind that is Aaron's favorite food of all times.

Nevertheless, this time the boys did not go for it and they offered up their next top two favorite restaurants, which Rob and I both shot down. Too much of the same! I felt like having Mexican, but Rob didn't. We were at a total loss for ideas, even though Southern California has more restaurants and fast food options than sand on the beach.

Finally, they suggested a Chinese fast food, which at least advertises that they don't use MSG. Okay, better! We went, and I looked through the buffet, thinking that I might at least have rice, which I really didn't want. But the main course options consisted of a variety of meats and vegetables, all of which were either marinated in soy sauce, teriyaki sauce or contained chicken!!

Really, there was not a single item I could have!!

I went to the restroom, and when I came out, Rob and the boys were already sitting at the table eating. I sat down and watched.

It was a very sad and lonely feeling.

I came home and drowned my sorrow in corn chips and mango salsa. Then Rob scolded me for eating junk food! Oh, the irony!!!

Day 189 – *Feeling of the Day*: Splendid

A great day today! Sushi lunch!!! Down two packs of soy sauce, only six months and 176 packs of soy sauce left!!! ☺

And dinner was just plain fantastic! I am delighted because I had enough time to whip up a very nice meal from all things in my fridge: I stir-fried green bell pepper, yellow squash and mushrooms, plenty of them! I filled that into a gluten-free tortilla, added some mango salsa, ham for protein and avocado for brain food. It was delicious and filling. I am so very happy with it!!

But as promised, today on Good Friday, I also ate my mixed berry pie. I couldn't even finish that piece, so there's more for tomorrow. Topped off with a little espresso (which is why I am writing this at nearly midnight). Too good!

I only cheated a wee bit when I ate three little chocolate eggs (my favorite Easter candy) that happen to sit in a little bowl on my side board in the living room. In fact, they kind of jump into my way each time I pass by and I always deflect the attack, but today came out of nowhere, I got hit! Right in my face! Aaah, the taste is still with me! "Next year," I keep thinking. "Next year!"

Day 190 – *Feeling of the Day*: **Fat**

Aaaaaaaaand I gained a pound over yesterday's meal(s)!!!

Day 191 – *Feeling of the Day*: Detached

Easter Sunday. Boy, does the rest of the family have eggs to eat!! They better get to it because I won't be helping this year.

Day 192 – *Feeling of the Day*: Going downhill

Status update! Really not a happy camper. I've been breaking out again during the last week. Now, I've also felt as if my finger joints on my right hand were a bit swollen when waking up for the past two to three days. Not really bad but it makes me wonder what's going on now.

And then on top of that, last night I felt my gum inflammation reoccur. This one is super annoying! It's the bottom left side of the jaw, and even though it's mild, it's not great. The gums are slightly swollen and they're a bit more sensitive.

Let me see, however, how long it's been since the last time . . . gotta look back at my notes here . . . Yup, found it! Roughly three months ago.

Well, that's not bad, but not great. I hope this one will stay local and go away soon!

I really wonder why all these things are coming up together. Could it have anything to do with mishaps of last week? Am I really that sensitive to those foods now?

Questions running wild! I'll be seeing Doc for my last IV today! YAY!! Will ask him all those questions!

Day 194 – *Feeling of the Day*: Learning depressing things

Well, the gum inflammation is still there, still in the same place and hasn't gotten worse. It's sensitive, but I can brush my teeth and floss. Before, when this happened, the pain was excruciating and I could only brush the teeth ever so carefully, avoiding any contact with the gum! This is not like that at all. I just hope, it'll go away soon and not spread around like it used to.

No swollen fingers in the morning anymore either, so that's better. And not really breaking out. All in all, things are looking up and I've been eating well.

Last Monday's IV went well. Twinkle sweet talked my vein into cooperating and ended up using one that pops out on my wrist! On my wrist!!!

It was weird to look at it. I didn't dare move my hand even though Twinkle said I could totally relax and let my hand drop. I didn't. Twinkle laughed and then gently moved my fingers because I was holding my hand out like a claw, afraid that this thing would pop out if I moved anything out of place.

But it worked and Doc and Twinkle got a good laugh out of my death grip of a fictitious ball. Glad to have provided the entertainment for the day.

The only downside to Monday's visit was the contents of an article that I read. It was about cooking methods. I found that roasting food in the oven and using the microwave is detrimental to the nutrition in the food and should really be avoided.

Extreme high heat and flash heating, barbequing and other methods of browning of the food all produce a combination of sugars and another chemical byproduct that is harmful, too. On top of that, you'll be developing a taste for sweets, basically looking for it in all meals. Artificial sweeteners are no good either (but I already knew that). Nothing was really good.

Safest thing seems to be to stop eating. No, wait, not a solution!

I read another article about glaucoma and how sugar is bad for that as well. So, I went home and had coffee, cookies and some dark chocolate, thinking about how bad that is. I thought about it for a long time.

Day 195 – *Feeling of the Day:* Discouraged

I think I had too many cookies. Or too much of something else, not sure. My belly is sticking out like there's no tomorrow. I went to my bedroom and my belly arrived a solid minute before me! What did I do? I don't want this! Should I go on a diet?

Nope! I'm already on a diet and it's already producing plenty of food panic in my house.

Ah, I do know, however, that we've been having dinner way too late. It's spring break, and some of our dinners did not come together until 8pm. And I also ate some raw food with those, even though, as I already know, those should be avoided after about 4pm. Dinner at 6pm. It's not happening.

Just wait for school to start up again next week. Back to routine, in my head at least for now!

Day 196 – *Feeling of the Day*: Mixed feelings

Gum inflammation is dying down, without having traveled to any other region in my mouth. It was a short and mild visit, glad about that!

When I wake up in the morning, I still feel as if my fingers are slightly swollen. I thought it was going away, but over the last couple of days, I'm feeling it again. I'll be watching and asking Doc about it next Monday. Not cool.

I need to cut down on sugar. ☹

Day 197 – *Feeling of the Day*: Very excited, until I messed up again

I am so excited, I found NEW food!!! This is super exciting because I had time to stroll around the health food store and check out more stuff. I found food bowls!! Great mixes with different flavors, like chickpea curry, Mediterranean tempeh, and Southwestern quinoa and black bean mix. There were five flavors in all, but one contained chicken and one other had sesame seeds, so those two were out. But three new meals, this is great! I also dared buying a kale veggie burger and some dairy-free soy ice cream!!

The original plan was for me to get pea milk and one other thing, but I walked out $110 later! Nevertheless, I am happy because I needed some new ideas. I came home with three bags full to the brim, and hubby asked if I was doing okay. "Yes!" I shouted, "I'm great!! I have new food!!! For meeeeee!!!!"

It was a good day!!! ☺

Late evening:

So many opportunities for messing up; so little time! I was good today, really, I was! I had dinner at 7pm and nothing after until I sat with Lucas who had his dinner a little later today. I'd had some corn earlier in the day; therefore, today is declared a 'corn day' and I figured this is my chance to have some corn chips! Just a few more.

And even later, Rob suggested we take Lucas out for ice cream, since Aaron was at a friend's birthday party and Lucas needed some attention. Of course, I didn't have any ice cream (even though I wanted some so badly!). I ended up having a soy cappuccino (it's still not that good!), and now I feel really full. Again! ☹ Tummy sticking out! I shouldn't have had it!

It might help if I just brush my teeth right after dinner! I am too lazy to do it twice per night, so I think if I had brushed my teeth that would have stopped me from having the coffee. But I am too weak to say "No!" when I should. Yes, I'm a weakling! What can I do?

Day 198 – *Feeling of the Day:* Missing the mark

The 'no chocolate' thing didn't work out for me today! ☹

I'll try again tomorrow!

Day 199 – *Feeling of the Day*: Finally, some joy

Today is my last IV! I'm feeling nostalgic... NOOOOOT!!

It's been twelve weeks in a row, getting poked, having stuff pulled out of my bones and fat, and as the all-out highlight of the series, I get to pee in the bucket today. Not only once, but each time I need to go for six hours following the IV in order to collect a representative sample of eliminated heavy metals, which will be sent to the lab. What an ordeal!

Ok, fine, it's not really a bucket, but I must collect pee in a container that looks a lot like a container for gas that I would take to the gas station. Probably the same maker, thinking 'Diversify'!

All of this also cost me a good amount of $$, but that's okay. I just hope the final lab will show that most of it is gone and I don't have to continue in order to be at normal levels.

Crossing my fingers and toes starting now!

Later in the evening:

Still peeing in the bucket. One more time and I'm done for today. Then, bottle up the specimen and mail it out.

Bitter-sweet thing – I'll miss my Monday-Twinkle! ;)

Will not miss poking my veins each week!

Also, Doc and I talked briefly about where to go from here. The results from the pee test should hopefully come back by the beginning of next week, and we'll go from there. But Doc said today, "Don't expect your headaches to come back!"

That was one of the nicest things he could have said to me!!

Even later in the evening:

I am finally starting to feel good about today. No celebratory feelings earlier for as long as I had to collect specimen. Also, I had no chocolate or cookies today, so that made for a blah coffee time. Just had some fruit and then went on to cook a super healthy dinner (for myself). Veggie stir-fry that I filled into a gluten-free wrap. Pasta for the rest of the fam.

Finally!! I am done doing my "you-know-what" in the bucket, and at last, I am starting to feel relieved! I'm happy! I can smile!! I don't even care that I can't mail it out tonight (it's too late in the evening), and therefore, I have a pee sample in my fridge! Lovely!!

Oh no! I just realized, I brushed my teeth, but I must drink one more powder drink! ☹   Bummer!! What did I say about brushing my teeth twice in the evening?!?!!

Day 200 – *Feeling of the Day*: Liberated and happy

It's so liberating to pee freely without having to aim for the collection cup! Never knew that I would appreciate this so much one day. Liberty and justice for all!

I had my last of all last powder drinks tonight. Remember, there were three drinks each day of the IV and three drinks the day after. That makes for six drinks per IV, 12 IVs, therefore 72 powder drinks over the course of the last three months. Not tasty and I had to take my time so that I wouldn't get stomach cramps again.

I am so happy to be done! I felt GREAT all day! I even got two very nice compliments during my morning walk from strangers, commenting on the fact that I looked great and radiated happiness. And I truly feel that way today! I am super happy, feel free and healthier, even though I'm still pushing my tummy ahead of me. I got more energy and am looking forward to almost everything on my calendar, starting with coffee time with Victoria in the morning!

Life is good!

Late evening:

It was tango night tonight, but hubby was very tired, and I forgot to take my dance shoes along, so we decided to play hooky from tango and go out to dinner instead. I had already eaten beforehand, but I went along for the ride and a hot water with lemon.

Then Rob asked the one question I can't say no to, "Do you want an espresso?"

I couldn't say, "No", but at least I said, "Nnnnnnnn" and ended up having half an espresso. I guess that counts as progress! Right?

Day 202 – *Feeling of the Day*: Perplexed

The weirdest thing just happened! I had breakfast and a little while later, my face got really red and hot. I could feel it before I even went to check in the mirror! I don't know what's going on, and I feel a little strange, too! My face got red all the way up to my ears! And a little bit on the neck, too.

I know last night's dinner wasn't great. We went to a Mexican fast food restaurant for a school fundraiser. At the time, I thought it was not bad at all. I had a veggie bowl with rice, black beans, grilled bell pepper, guacamole, salsa and salad with a few corn chips on the side. Should have been all good. Overnight, I felt heavy and it just sat there in my stomach for a while. Surprising because I had not had that kind of feeling in a very long time!

Then I woke up this morning, still feeling kind of full, but nothing else. No red face or anything.

For breakfast, I had my very mild (read: bland!) buckwheat-quinoa bread (that I baked myself) with some honey and banana and a rooibos tea.

Suddenly, I felt my face burning after cleaning up the breakfast table, and for a tiny little while, I even felt just a tad nauseous. And super tired. What the heck?!?!

If this is from last night's food at the restaurant, then why would this happen some 12-13 hours later? And my breakfast? Nothing dangerous here, I strongly believe that there wasn't anything bad in it.

Now, an hour later, still feeling it, still red-faced. I've never had a reaction like this ever before! I'll have to keep watching it. This is very puzzling!

Day 203 – *Feeling of the Day*: Trying to make an effort

Date day with Rob today (he works four ten-hour days, therefore, Friday he is home, and these are our date days.) Today went like this.

We went to work out, went for a massage, went for lunch, went for coffee, fought at the coffee shop, went home and made up, went to the market with Lucas, who came home shortly after (Aaron at a friend's house), will have dinner in a little while, and then go to Aaron's flag football game.

Full day!!

The fight was mostly about two things: 1. Not having family dinners (my fault), and 2. not communicating well (hubby's fault).

So, we're even; here's our plan for resolving the two issues. I will make family dinners for the days that Rob goes to work and comes home at 6:15pm or so. That's reasonable! Our dinners had become so scattered with my occasional efforts to make something for the whole family, and then, family not all liking it and wanting fish sticks or instant noodles instead. Rob usually cooks his own meat; he's big on that (and I never was), so it's all gone wayside.

I need to shape up and do better!!!

Rob suggested I make the family favorite, Mongolian Beef, once a week. It's a start; now I need three more dinners. Most importantly, Rob needs to like it, and the kids will have to learn to eat more variety. It's a beautiful picture in my head. Hope I can make that a reality.

Rob, on the other hand, will try to communicate better and let me know stuff. For example, if he's coming home later than usual or things that are going on at work (so we can have a conversation), etc.

I want the dinner conversation we see in the movies! I need to really, really work on it and not let it go. Really, really!

Day 204 – *Feeling of the Day*: Like Sherlock Holmes

I solved the mystery of the red face attack after breakfast a couple of days ago! I pulled out the buckwheat-quinoa bread again this morning to eat another slice, and after I ate about half of it, my lips started to feel kind of funny, and my skin got itchy. Real allergy symptoms this time! I looked at the bread more closely and thought that parts of it looked redder than others.

Lucas confirmed the red hue on parts of the bread, so I am sure that something in the bread must have gone bad.

I baked this bread initially with just a variety of flours (all-purpose, buckwheat and quinoa) and it came out kind of bland. The next time, I added chopped dates to give it more flavor. It came out bland with dates.

But I think it was the dates that had gone bad. Mystery solved and leftover bread tossed! ☹

Now, I'll have to bake another loaf of bread, and I might try one with other flours, not necessarily quinoa. Quinoa is one of the grains that had an evil star, so I'm only supposed to eat it maybe twice a week at the most. And making it one of my regular breakfast foods has increased the quinoa load in my meals greatly. Will try!

Hopefully, I'll bake something that I might even take to Germany with me when I go the week after next!

Day 205 – *Feeling of the Day*: Ecstatic!

H – A – L – F – T – I – M – E !!!!!!

I'm dancing! I'm prancing! I'm movin'! I'm groovin'!

Picture this: One-sided shoulder roll while snapping my fingers, walking backwards with a bounce,

Now shimmy, shimmy with the shoulders, lean forward and back!

YAY!!! It's halftime; only six months to go!!! Half time!! (Where's the show?)

I can't believe it's time for this!! It seems like forever since I received my no-go list of foods and tried to make this work! I clearly remember sitting at my dining table with Kate on the day I started grocery shopping for my new diet and almost crying on her shoulder. Now, I'm still alive and have healed several of my little aches and pains and learned lots of things. For example, tempeh is just another term for soy – sort of.

I made it through this far and now, I am looking downhill. It's a nice view from up here! So glad to have reached it!!

Halloween, here we come!!!

Day 206 – *Feeling of the Day*: Looking ahead

The first day of my second half of this ordeal! ☺ Nice to know, I have (almost) no problem feeding myself and learned to cook a few meals, too.

Of course, this second half is not without challenges. There will be some traveling, outside of the state as well as international. I'll have to figure those out and see what types of foods I will find.

The first trip is coming up in ten days. I'll be visiting my family in Germany for twelve days. I already started a list of things that I should bring, such as snacks and first day supplies and soy sauce packs.

At least, for part of the time, I'll be at either my mom's or dad's house, so I can cook. But I won't be allowed any of the good bread, cheese or chocolate. That's a major disappointment, but alas, I'll be back some time on another trip and eat full force! I am hopeful!

Day 207 – *Feeling of the Day*: Weary

OMG, this is taking foreeeeeeeeeeeverrrr!! Time is just dragging on!!!

I thought, the second half of this year would fly by. However, here I am; it's only 2:37pm on the second day of the second half, and the clock is not moving!

This is taking too long! I would like to be done. Now! Please!?!?!

Deep sigh!!!!

Day 208 – *Feeling of the Day*: A little too busy for comfort

Weird day today! It happened again; the fiery red face after I ate a slice of my own quinoa bread. I thought it should be fine because this one came straight out of the freezer. There should have been nothing wrong with it. So now, I dumped the whole lot including what I had left in the freezer, altogether about six or seven slices.

I don't know what caused the reaction, but I will be baking bread again, this time without dates. Maybe, they don't freeze well?

For lunch, I had some quinoa and root vegetables, but no reaction, so it's not the quinoa – it must be something else, but what?

It was a super busy day today; been running around all day until 6:30pm, when Lucas's soccer practice finished, got home and made dinner. I have a slight headache, not bad, but some pressure on the right back side. Why?!?

I didn't want to have a headache again! It's been so good without it! We've had crazy temperature changes over the past few days, from cool to hot in the daytime and back to cold, and I didn't even consider having a headache then. They were a thing of the past!

But today, slight reminder of what was once. I don't like it. I really wanted to watch some trashy TV tonight, but I just might have to go to bed early. ☹ Good night!

1 hour later:

Ha! I fended off the headache with an ice pack and a strong espresso!! Trash TV, here I come!! Life is good after all!!!

Day 209 – *Feeling of the Day*: A little let down

May, the Fourth, be with you! It's not; at least not as much as I hoped.

I received the lab results from my chelation treatment and although things have improved quite a bit, lead and aluminum have only been reduced by about 30 percent. These two are still in the red, aka 'outside of reference' level.

The report still says the following about my lead burden: "This individual's urine lead exceeds three times the upper expected limit per the reference population." Not good, is it now?

I'm glad most of the others are now in the yellow area, or even less, back in the green area which is 'within reference'. So, I should be happy; nevertheless, I'm a little disappointed about the lead. I thought I'd be done after this. I have so little experience in this area that I didn't expect it might take more to fix me.

On the other hand, I know and appreciate that the treatment has helped, and I am noticeably feeling better. It'd be great if I could improve even more. I don't know what I'll do with myself if I feel even better than this!!!

Doc had emailed the results to me, so I responded, asking what to do now. Waiting to hear from him.

10pm:

It's 10pm and I'm eating dessert! What the heck am I thinking?!?!!

I'm thinking that I wish my lead level was a lot lower than what it is! I'm eating because I'm frustrated. Great!! Next week is my 30-year high school reunion, and I need to be skinny and look as if I've got it all together!

Well, I do! I've got my tea, my dessert and my TV show all together, ready to make it a memorable night!

Day 210 – *Feeling of the Day*: Accepting

Doc called me and said that he was quite happy with the results. There was obviously quite an improvement in all the heavy metal readings. He thinks that from here on out we should give it a rest for now and retest in about three to six months.

He says that my liver is in much better shape now than what it was before; and therefore, better able to detoxify my body on its own. I must admit that makes sense.

So, for now, Doc says, he does not see the immediate need to do another six or twelve IVs but wait a while and see how things are going on their own.

Obviously when we retest, if the levels get worse again, then we'll have to go back to treatment and possibly look for sources of current and ongoing exposure (which at this point, I have no idea where lead and aluminum would come from).

Day 211 – *Feeling of the Day*: Burning

It happened again! The red face and burning feeling!! Why?!?!?

I had no breakfast but an early lunch of roasted root vegetables, mainly potatoes and carrots, and a corn and bean salad, both of which I'd eaten many times before. Never been a problem thus far.

After that, I took my vitamin D, B and my fish oil, which are all in liquid (oil) format. I felt the burning coming on strongly, right after I took that vitamin B (not my favorite taste in wanna-be-raspberry), so I think, the reaction may have come from that. But again, I've been using that supplement for quite a while and no problem ever!

The burning feeling lasted for a long time, almost all day! ☹ So weird!

The rest of the day was great though, with lots of fun. We went to see LA Galaxy; our local major league soccer team play against Chicago who had just recruited Germany's top dog Bastian Schweinsteiger!

It was awesome and so much more fun than I had even imagined! I took Aaron, Lucas and Lucas's best friend. We had such a great time! Came home very late, however, and desperately needed sleep!

Day 212 – *Feeling of the Day*: Grumpy

This weekend has been so busy! It's finally time to rest a little and get my head wrapped around the fact that I'll be leaving for Germany in three days and to plan out the things that I still need to do before I leave!

And then, of course, what happens this morning? Headache!

Really?!?!?!! Is this really necessary??? Headache, I don't need you; let's split up!

I had three big glasses of water and took a mild pain medicine, but that didn't help. After breakfast, I rested and put an icepack on my head. Didn't do the trick either. I finally succumbed to taking half a real painkiller, had lunch, and it's oooookayyyy, but not really gone yet. I've been nauseous, too. That hasn't happened in a while. Pretty sure, I'm not pregnant.

Maybe coffee will help!

Boys are watching *Guardians of the Galaxy* at a very loud volume; that's not really doing me any good either.

I also still have that burning feeling in my face from yesterday. I refrained from taking any of the oil-based vitamins this morning. I was so afraid the burning would come back. Now, after lunch, I only took the fish oil for omega-3s. I feel the burn, just slightly, but then, altogether, I'm not doing really well today. ☹

Argh, just not happy today. ☹☹

Day 214 – *Feeling of the Day*: Joy

Since I lost most of my Sunday to that stupid headache, I've had to cut down my to-do list by a few items, simply because it is TOMORROW that I am leaving for Germany! I'm nervous about the food situation, but I am sooo excited to go!

Ten days with my parents, my brother and his family for a few days, and then seeing my high school friends!! And, of course, my best friend in Germany, Mia, whom I have known since I was two!! I can't wait!!

It's time to pack! I have one large suitcase that is full of clothes and gifts. And my small roller case as my carry-on is full of odd snacks, consisting of bean and rice chips, roasted chickpeas, salted fava beans, protein bars made from pea protein and rice, fava bean cereal. It's gonna be interesting opening the luggage at customs, if I have too! ☺

But who cares?!? I'm excited!!!!! Yay, Deutschland!

Day 215 – *Feeling of the Day*: Sufficiently Prepared

First day of travel – Here we go; this is exciting! I am on my way to Germany to see my family and friends. Actual kick-off to this trip was my upcoming 30-year high school reunion. I haven't seen anyone in 30 years over there, and I am really looking forward to it! I had some nice classmates and it will be great to see them again.

I hope I will discover new food variations, suitable to my diet plan! ☺

I had a very safe breakfast at home, a lovely and also safe lunch at the health food store with hubby on the way to the airport and now, I'm in the airplane, off I go. . .

Nutritional free fall!!

Being naturally organized, however, I am prepared to avoid famine during the next 20 or so hours of total travel time. My carry-on luggage holds the following safety-net food items:

Corn chips, my favorite gluten-free sandwich cookies, purple heirloom potato chips with coconut oil (interesting, but not my personal favorite), a banana (I better eat that before the London layover), roasted fava beans, salted chickpeas and chips made from beans and lentils. Don't ask! I haven't tried them yet.

The dinner on the airplane wasn't bad. I had pre-ordered a vegetarian meal. I was able to eat about one half of it. You only have one choice when ordering a special meal for the flight; it's either gluten-free, free of dairy, kosher or vegetarian or vegan.

Apparently, people with multiple allergies or food restrictions across those categories don't fly or they don't eat during a flight.

Out of ten hours of flight into London Heathrow, just seven more to go – Still got my banana!

I watched a movie, got up to stretch and pee, tried to sleep, 6:31 hours to go!

5:47 more hours to go.

This is painful!

Day 216 – *Feeling of the Day*: British

Second Day of Travel – I'm in London for a six-hour layover in Heathrow! I'm not really free-falling food-wise yet because I'm still living off my own snacks. But I enjoyed a very nice coffee with 'soya' milk!

Yes, the British are so very elegant that 'elevator' is 'lift', 'apartment' is 'flat', 'vacation' is 'holiday' and now 'soy' is 'soya'!

It was delicious, mainly because I'm halfway delirious with fatigue. It's 3:20pm local time, and I must stay awake at least another three hours to board my connecting flight. But it is 7:20am in my body and I only had about 2 hours of sleep on the long flight.

The coffee also disqualified me immediately from possibly being considered a local since Heathrow is all things tea! I'm entertaining the thought of replacing all my dish towels from home because they have lots of whimsical or cool, London-style, British-flag ones here AND they are called 'tea towels'!

Another 1½ hours before my next connection. I'm watching British Airways galore outside!

Bloody marvelous!

Day 217 – *Feeling of the Day*: Calm before the storm

At my Mom's!! I'm so happy! ☺ We're going to have a big fat day of no plans today, just what I wanted. The schedule will start rolling over me beginning tomorrow, but today, we are FREE!

We had a great lunch, one of my favorite seasonal meals of white asparagus, peeled and cooked for about 20 minutes with a pinch of sugar and salt each, yellow potatoes boiled in salt water, and fresh, thick slices of black forest ham.

That's all, so simple and so very tasty!

The only thing that usually goes with it (not for me right now), is the butter sauce that is browned in the pan and thickened with breadcrumbs. That sauce is what got me eating asparagus and cauliflower as a child (starting with more sauce than veggies). However today, I didn't need it! Lunch was perfect and I want to eat it at least two more times before I leave, since it's the season, the asparagus season!

Coffee time was filled with fruit and a couple of my own cookies that I had brought. Nothing special here, but I found a vegan, gluten-free, non-dairy creamer at the supermarket this morning! It comes in sealed single portions and is made of palm oil, dextrose, glucose syrup, emulsifiers, starch and stabilizers. There is a bunch of numbers on the list of ingredients, which is usually not a good or natural thing, but I can travel with these! It comes in a 10-pack; I bought four of them.

But now, I'm thinking, "Hmmm, summer travel is coming up! At least two trips are planned and not sure what I'll find over there. I shall go back to the market and buy at least twelve more 10-packs!"

I will survive!!

My summer travel check list in order of priority (so far): Passport, ticket, credit card, coffee creamer, xylitol, bathing suit! Yay!!

Totally doable ☺

Day 218 – *Feeling of the Day*: Indulging

I left my Mom's house this morning to spend the weekend with my brother and his family. In order to celebrate our get-together, my sister-in-law had prepared a seasonal delicacy for lunch consisting of white asparagus, potatoes and black forest ham. GREAT!

I shared my cookies for coffee time, and they all liked them!

Tonight is my 30-year high school reunion and I cannot wait to see all my friends from ages ago! It'll be great!!

Day 219 – *Feeling of the Day*: Blissful

Today was the church confirmation of Mia's daughter. I am glad I made it in time despite the reunion last night. It was phenomenal, and the last few of us classmates stayed up talking and laughing together until 3am!

The best thing about it was that it didn't turn into a popularity contest, but genuine interest in what everyone had become and made out of their lives. So many different paths, and yet, some things had not changed at all (Jacob, still late to the occasion, as usual)! ;)

Short night, but fabulous!!

I reached the rustic restaurant for today's confirmation celebration while all the guests were still gathering in the front, congratulating the young lady, Person of the Day! Eventually, we went inside to enjoy a fantastic lunch, as chosen by the Person of the Day. We had a seasonal delicacy of white asparagus, rounded off with potatoes, ham, and also some salmon. I had all of it and loved it!

To get to all these events, I've been cruising over the Autobahn left and right. I love to drive out here! I went steadily around 100mph. My Mom's car is 17 years old and I don't want to push it too hard. I know exactly when to move over from one lane to the other if I want to pass a slower car, but not break my speed or the speed of the faster cars approaching from behind. One second you see a dot in the distance far behind you, and next thing you know that dot turned into a car nearly sitting on your rear axle.

I've been having so much fun driving, I almost missed my exit today! There will be more driving tomorrow. I'm going into former East Germany with my Dad!

Day 220 – *Feeling of the Day*: Paying for yesterday's bliss

I woke up with a light headache this morning, pressure on the back of the head, right-hand side. I know I didn't drink enough water yesterday. It was busy and it got really warm. Also, I had only had those 4½ hours of sleep the night before (after the reunion).

Today, Dad and I are going to the Eastern part of Germany for a quick two-day excursion. Our first destination will be the city of Leipzig. It will take us about 3 hours of driving to get there.

All these events may be adding to that nagging pressure in the back of my head. I already drank three 12oz glasses of water this am, hoping to make up for yesterday. The question is how many pee stops can one make on a 3½ hour drive without turning it into a day trip?!

Day 222 – *Feeling of the Day*: Enlightened with historical treasures

I am sitting on my Mom's balcony, having breakfast (rice bread, which I carried wIth me from CA) with peanut butter and jelly. It feels as if it's been forever since I wrote my last bit two days ago, sitting in this very same spot. But that was before the trip and this is right after!

We had an awesome time! My headache disappeared over the course of the morning; no pill needed! ☺

The city of Leipzig is beautiful! We arrived just in time for lunch after securing two hotel rooms right smack in the city center within walking distance to many sights. We spent the entire rest of the afternoon strolling through the old city center, looking at beautiful buildings that have been restored after WWII. We saw part of the modern university that incorporates the remaining front of an old church, which had been destroyed during the war. We saw the gigantic central train station and dotted all those visits with coffee at a local bakery/café and dinner at the Brazilian steakhouse. Fabulous!!

Everybody has soy creamer, so I didn't need my most excellent artificial take-along coffee creamer at all! Also, I learned that I can still go to the bakery with my Dad for coffeetime – an essential quality time necessity – and pick out a pie that has fruit in gelatin on top of the crust. Then, I just eat the fruit-gelatin part of it and pretend to be enjoying it just as much as the whole pie!

However, after asking about breakfast options, the nice lady behind the bakery counter came up with nothing and therefore had no issue heating up my gluten-free buckwheat waffle that had traveled with me from CA as my back-up plan.

I still ordered tea and a fruit salad to make her feel better (and myself, too)!

Seems like no issues traveling at all – as long as there is a Plan B in my purse! ☺

Yesterday, the second day of our little trip, we visited one more monument and then moved on to Eisenach, where we got to see the fortress called Wartburg.

This is where Martin Luther had found shelter and protection while translating the bible from Latin into German language so that the common people could read it for themselves (the ones who knew how to read).

The fortress is fantastic; we wandered around for nearly two hours and still hadn't even gone into the exhibits inside. It felt as if we were in a fairy tale fortress with its tall tower, the courtyard and the dovecot. That is, until I went up the smaller tower and about half way up, I stepped out from the landing into one small square opening in the tower, found the hole in the ground covered with an iron gate, which lead by direct fall into the dungeon. I quickly retreated, unnoticed, and went on to explore coffeetime options with my Dad in the various yards.

Coffee, yes; but no cake in sight for me, so I ended up picking the fruit out of Dad's cake.

Finally, we got on our way home. It was a three-hour drive. We got there around 8pm and my stepmom had made the perfect dinner as a conclusion to the perfect trip with a seasonal delicacy of white asparagus, potatoes and ham!

I was so touched because everybody has been trying to spoil me and serve up the best food of the season! I will never get tired of this meal! I am loving it!

Day 223 – *Feeling of the Day*: Treading carefully

Shucks! I have my old gum inflammation flaring up on the right-hand side in the far back, inside and outsides of the gum, plus a small white spot on the inside of my cheek. This is not as bad as it could be, but definitely more irritated than the last time.

Why?

I've been eating the right foods, but, of course, I've been eating out a lot while traveling. There's also been just the slightest offense in food repetition (think the seasonal delicacy). In addition, I've been eating much less fresh fruit or salads, no legumes, mainly due to lack of control over the food choices available during travel and visits.

If this happens again, I shall watch the food intake and compare to these notes.

Oh, and I've had too little sleep. Wonder why?!? Mommy's out partying!!

Day 224 – *Feeling of the Day*: Very, very grateful

The gum inflammation is already dying down. It's still sensitive when brushing teeth, but much less than yesterday. The little white spot inside of my cheek is gone as well.

Today was a great day! Lots of 'no schedule' on the agenda! Even though it's been really fun to visit with my family and friends over the last few days, it was a perfect day today back home with Mom and no plans.

This left plenty of time for us to go buy all the ingredients to make a very special lunch, just one more time – a seasonal delicacy!

Mom and I peeled the asparagus together and I watched the seasoning and boiling process, just so I could make it, too, if I ever found white asparagus in CA.

After lunch, we went for a walk through the park nearby. This park is very large (although not even the biggest in Hanover). There are wild deer, stags, and boars inside a large enclosure with many piglets fighting and playing in the dirt.

The mature chestnut trees are enormous and in full bloom. Walking through the park is like walking through a green tunnel, spotting small herds of deer resting under the trees, even as pedestrians walk by.

The fresh air filled my lungs with life and my eyes couldn't get enough of the many shades of green as we walked on. With all the fun I've been having and all the socializing I've been doing, this was like the meditating piece of the vacation.

I feel so thankful!

Day 225 – *Feeling of the Day*: Full of energy

Gum inflammation is gone! ☺ And my life is back to all good and healthy! Since my arrival, I have not gained one bit of weight, my energy level is high and I feel really, really good! Of course, I'm on vacation with my family; it's easy to re-energize this way.

My Mom's condo is on the 7th floor in a large building. I always take the stairs to go up and down. Today, however, I took two steps at a time all the way up to her place.

Later in the day, Mom and I drove to my brother's house, roughly 55 miles from Hanover, for coffee and a BBQ dinner. His mother-in-law and brother-in-law were there as well. We ate like kings and queens! Delicious salads, meat and grilled veggies. Everyone who contributed to the meal was trying to accommodate my food restrictions. I am so touched!

We stayed until almost midnight and then drove home. It was a very relaxed visit, but then also time to say good-bye because I'm flying home to Los Angeles in two days.

Dang it! (Only because I must leave my family here behind again in order to see my own boys and my husband!)

Day 226 – *Feeling of the Day*: Blue

It's my last day in Germany today. I am so sad to leave my parents. I was sitting across from my Mom during lunch yesterday and while she was talking, I was thinking about how much I love her and wish I could do this regularly, sharing a meal with her.

Today, I used the morning hours to pack and then went to a fabulous Greek restaurant for lunch with both my parents. Even though they are divorced, they are still friends and live very close to each other, so this works out.

Lunch was fantastic: Gyro meat, tomato rice, thick French fries, cabbage salad with a clear vinegar and oil dressing. YUM!!

The menu contained all the details as to what allergens were present in the respective meals. I could say that travelling and eating here in Germany with food restrictions has not been a problem at all!

Especially since I carried some snacks with me, I never got in trouble being hungry and then panic that I would not have any food available to me. I am leaving some of the snacks, cookies and chocolate behind for my Mom, my niece and sister-in-law. Everyone LOVES my snacks! ☺

Tomorrow – It's time to go to the airport, head back over to London and then Los Angeles.

I miss my boys very much, and Rob, of course, but I am really sad to leave my parents and the rest of the family. My heart wants to live in two places at the same time!

Day 227 – *Feeling of the Day*: Longing for my boys

I am in London, déjà-vu! On the approach to landing at Heathrow, we flew over the city and I saw Tower Bridge and Buckingham Palace CLEARLY! It was a most splendid view! However, there was no royalty out on the balcony waving at our plane up above, and I must ask, "Why?? Brexit?!? I didn't do it!"

In any case, Heathrow provides a superb selection of foods for the wary traveler. I chose a natural foods restaurant with Middle Eastern inspired food. Every food choice was clearly marked as either gluten-free, wheat-free, vegetarian, vegan etc. Bloody fantastic!!

After a tasty okra and sweet potato falafel lunch, I strolled through the stores, mainly Harrod's. I saw a beautiful fine bone china coffee mug in pale blue and white with gold swirls. The mug wanted to come home with me. I tried telling it that I couldn't take it; I already have a serious collection of mugs at home! The mug didn't want to hear it and called my name until it became embarrassing and I finally conceded. The mug is coming to America with me and just for good measure, I purchased one of the 50 or so tea selections as well.

Seriously, I couldn't help it! It wasn't my fault!!

I texted Rob and my boys that I'm about to board the next flight and I'll see them in roughly 13 hours. I only cried for a short while after the text. I am really missing them.

Day 228 – *Feeling of the Day*: Mainly hungry

So, back to disaster... I mean, back home ;)

The house is still standing, the boys are alive and everything else looks fine, too. I was very happy to see my family of course, especially Lucas hugged me so tight, he did not want to let go of me when I first saw everybody at the airport. It was so very sweet! I didn't want to let go either.

It was evening when I arrived, so we only had a couple of hours before I thought I was going to keel over backwards with exhaustion. Nevertheless, I made it through the first night with hardly any disruptions and got up at the regular time following local time, trying to keep jetlag at bay.

Lunch, however, was a whole different story. I hadn't had a chance yet to go grocery shop today. Instead, there was unpacking, laundry and some tidying up to do. When I got really hungry, I realized it was lunchtime, but I had no real food on hand. I checked through the freezer and found some quinoa which boils quickly. Perfect! No vegetables at home, though, so I thought, I'll just add some fruit to my meal for vitamins. I cut up an orange while cooking the quinoa.

Unfortunately, I didn't think about how quinoa, lightly salted, would taste in orange juice when served on the same plate as orange pieces. Turns out, it doesn't taste that great. What a lunch! I topped it off with some mango that was still in the fridge from before I left on my trip.

Wow, I must go grocery shopping tomorrow!!

Best part of this day so far? Fabulous coffee in my new mug from London Heathrow, so elegant!

1 hour later:

I'm hungry! Who knew that salted orange quinoa was so unfulfilling?!?

Day 229 – *Feeling of the Day*: Apprehensive

Dinner is bound to be a catastrophe! I can feel it! Hubby sprang a light-hearted, "Why don't you make something in the crockpot for tonight?" on me. I chipperly answered, "Sure! I'll look through the recipes, and oh, look what I found? A simple beef stew!"

So, out I went, first for a doctor's appointment (just my annual check-up, should be fine) and then to go grocery shopping. I hit the big wholesale store and the nearest health food store. I got everything except for the beef. They didn't have the right kind, and I knew that the other health food store closer to my home has a great selection, so off I went!

Quick stop at home, though, to put freezer and fridge items away and then I went out again to get that meat. Sure enough, the nice man at the meat counter had the right kind and the right amount. The only problem now was timing.

The recipe book calls for 8-10 hours of cooking on low. It did not, however, give me the option of cooking for 4-5 hours on high as it does on other recipes. Hmmm?

I asked the nice man at the meat counter about it, and he said, that he would only cook the meat for about 5-6 hours on low. Now, I am adding about ½ pound to the amount of meat to be sure I have enough (Aaron's friend will stay for dinner with us today), so does this mean it cooks longer? He thought still about 5-6 hours. Add a little bit of water to make sure the potatoes and carrots get soft, he says.

By the time I came home, it was 11:45am and I still had to peel and cut the potatoes, carrots and onion, and it wasn't until 12:23pm that I was able to close the lid and start the cooker.

Now what? Cook on high for a shorter amount of time or cook on low and we won't be eating until tomorrow.

Neither the instruction manual for the cooker nor the book of recipes enlightened me about the option of mixing and matching times.

I resorted to setting the cooker on high, will leave it there for three hours and then go to the low setting for maybe another 2 hours or so.

I'm afraid dinner will be a disaster. My poor boys will probably wish I had stayed in Germany just a little bit longer! ☹

Day 230 – *Feeling of the Day*: Getting sick

Ok, dinner was not a disaster. Turns out that my timing of three hours on high and a little less than two hours on low cooking was just right for the meat to be cooked and tender, but not be dissolving just yet.

I stress too much over these little things, I guess. And dinner went just fine; everyone ate at least a plate full! So there!

Unfortunately, I started feeling a little under the weather last night, and today, I am full-blown sick with a bad cold, body aches, headache, and low-grade fever.

I remember, there were a LOT of people coughing in the airplane, so it might just be from that. I'm staying in bed and not doing much of anything. I'm not even capable of doing anything today, really.

Dinner will be whatever hubby can come up with. I love my husband!

Day 231 – *Feeling of the Day*: Daydreaming

I think it's not that I'll learn how to cook over this whole 'no food' experience. My real secret weapon is how to find a multitude of adequate snacks! It's the salted fava beans, purple heirloom potato chips cooked in coconut oil and popped bean crunch that keeps me up and alive.

I figured that if I ever wanted to eat healthy, real food that's good for me as well as my family and feed them right, I'll just have to hire a cook!! Not likely to happen, but it's a thought. A dream! Okay, utopia! Still, it's there!

Day 233 – *Feeling of the Day*: A little more Zen-like

I spent three days in bed with this fever! Not cool!! I had no appetite and hardly ate anything at all, so my diet is going well! ☺

No, really, I am feeling super weak today, but at least I got up again. I had about a half plate of lunch and a half can of lentil soup for dinner, one orange in the afternoon. That's more than I ate the previous two days combined. Getting better; I will eat a cow tomorrow!

Now, I did have a lot of time to think back about my trip and the food choices I had to make. Suddenly, I really miss German food! It seems lighter to me, but that may be because I grew up with it and it feels more natural to my body.

And as much as I have come to resort to Mexican or Asian foods as easy gluten-free choices (hold the cheese), I had a multitude of choices over there as well. There's an abundance of Greek and Turkish restaurants that have been there since I was little girl, and their food is perfect for my diet plan, no adaptations needed!

So, traveling is absolutely doable with a few things to keep in mind:

- Do a little bit of prep work. Bring snacks or treats, just in case, so you know you have something familiar to fall back on in case you really need it
- Have an open mind. Do not look to find the same thing you know from home, instead try local foods and restaurants and think about how you can adapt those foods
- Do not obsess over food variety and rotation of foods. Just go with the flow and the reduced level of stress will do you well (this is where I struggle the most, trying to be too perfect with my rotating)!

All in all, this trip to Germany was really good and I learned to relax a bit more again. Not that I'm compromising my food choices, but to stop obsessing and writing down each day's food items.

So, what if I eat rice two days in a row? So do about one billion plus people all over Asia! It's all good. Let's live a little!

Day 235 – *Feeling of the Day*: Unsatisfied

Well, that didn't work out for me! Hubby came home last night from being gone the whole long weekend and said, "Let's go to dinner!" The boys cheered, "Let's go to Islands Fine Burgers & Drinks!" I said, "Let's try something new!"

Of course, after quick and decisive eyebrow-raising on my part, hubby agreed that we could possibly try something new, and so we began to Yelp our way to a final decision on a new Chinese restaurant not too far from home. The boys were less than excited at this point, but I thought we'd have a chance to find some new foods this way.

The pictures and reviews were promising, so hubby agreed and off we went!

Well, the orders were made and reflected the same as what we would be ordering at the Chinese fast food: Kung Pao chicken, Orange chicken and dumplings. Only my dish was a new creation of Tofu in orange sauce.

Since the regular dish has tofu breaded and deep-fried and I required a gluten-free version, the waitress suggested I have the regular, soft tofu steamed and served in the sauce. I thought that was a marvelous idea, and she went to put in the order.

The food started rolling in, and it was plentiful, but hubby really didn't like the Kung Pao chicken. Too salty! Twice!! (After returning it the first time, the second plate was no better!)

The orange chicken was so abundant, it took over the table, and my tofu was served with nothing but sauce, no vegetables at all. I was hungry! The tofu was so soft, it practically slipped down my throat. I ended up eating too quickly and too much and felt sick for a while after.

But I couldn't admit it because the idea of trying something new was my fault. But really, how many stupid or clumsy food choices can one person alone make? Is it only me??

Please... anybody else in this with me??

Day 238 – *Feeling of the Day*: Weak

Oh man! I am still weak from being sick. This is no joke! I had to lay down for a nap in the afternoon yesterday. Food choices not mention-worthy; I am eating what I find at home ranging from packaged split pea soup to rice crackers. When I stopped finding stuff, I finally made a run to the store. I was mostly missing vegetables, so I went to the market and loaded up in good faith that I'll soon be preparing yummy dishes again – full of nutrition and taste.

I'm still waiting for this to happen. Well, I did make salad along with my lunch, so it's not all sad and sorrowful.

I also had to go to the home goods store, which is in the same shopping center as the market. I'm so weak! I ended up driving from one to the other. This is pathetic!

That would never happen in real life! I'd be the one hauling all my purchases from one store to the next for the sake of exercise! Yup, I'm that full of it! I mean normally full of energy!

But not now.

Going back to bed now. It's 2:45pm and I have an hour before the boys are coming home. And then there's a boys' chorus performance this evening. I'll have to stay upright for that because both Aaron and Lucas are in it and I'll have to try and not cough through the whole thing.

Day 240 – *Feeling of the Day*: Hopeful

It's Sunday, I'm starting to cough a little less. Well, maybe; only interrupted the pastor during the sermon once. Maybe I'll live.

I am living off yesterday's Mexican grill lunch leftovers, which I combined with my pasta leftovers from last week. I'll have the rice and beans leftovers for dinner. Voilà! Meal plan complete for the day!

The rest of the family? SOS (Search or Starve), as a friend of mine calls it!

Later in the afternoon:

Grrrrrrr! I'm so tired of vanilla coconut coffee creamer! It's just ruining my coffee time! Maybe it has to do with still being sick. Everything made me nauseous, even water for heaven's sake! Uggh!

On another note, though, I just realized I should check to see if I might be done with my second attempt at being gluten-free. Remember, Doc had given me the "Start all over, but now go gluten-free for four months" after it came out that I had been following my own guidelines on eating gluten-free, and they were no good!

Let's see, when did I start over?

Now, look at that! It was February 9th when I found out I had to redo my GF time, so I'm almost there!! Doc had told me, "Four months, longer is better." I chose to ignore the second part of his statement and will go with the four-months rule.

This is exciting, I'll be contacting Doc sometime this coming week to ask what I should be doing. Maybe there is a Big Day of Wheat coming my way after all! (Last time that one didn't happen because I had messed up for three months.)

Can't wait!

Day 242 – *Feeling of the Day:* Almost strong again

Yes!! My strength is coming back after being so sick! This morning I woke up and felt as if I could pull trees from the ground!!

Then I went for a walk and the strength dwindled.

Well, maybe I could pull one tree; something like bamboo.

Or maybe flowers? Let me think about it. Perhaps just grass? Yes, I can do grass!

Day 243 – *Feeling of the Day*: Sorry for Hubby

Hubby is sick with a bad, bad cold. Oh no, here we go again! Extra vitamin C dosages, zinc and the whole spiel. This is no fun. I want to move back to Hawaii now, breathe fresh air, hike in nature, drink clean spring water, wear grass skirts and a coconut bra, and have birds and butterflies circle my head all day long! Yes, that's the life!!

Well, we'll be going there, at least for this summer vacation, leaving in less than three weeks. Soooo looking forward to it! Cough. Cough.

Day 245 – *Feeling of the Day*: On a mission

I've been on a mission to find new dishes. I've really kind of been thinking about it for a year because our set is 21 years old (we got it for our wedding.) There are many chipped pieces, missing plates and the other plates have lots of scratches now, it just doesn't look so nice anymore.

But instead of going to the store just like that, now I am looking for something that is lead and cadmium free! It seems I can't just go and buy anything now. I did some research online and there are some specific brands that several sites recommend, but I'm just wondering when did life become so complicated?? Why can't I just go and buy dishes??

I went to several stores today to check out the selections and didn't even find anything that I really liked because it's not the dishes, it's me!

I want the dinnerware sets to be for everyday use, but nice enough to bring out for guests (my kitchen is small, and I really don't have space for two separate sets of dishes). Also, I don't want the dishes to be heavy. I don't need mugs, I prefer coffee cups with a saucer, and of course, I must like the color or pattern.

And lead and cadmium free! Not too much to ask, is it?

Well, it seems so.

For one thing, I know that the dishes of one of the housewares store nearby seem to adhere to strict standards regarding heavy metal use in the glazes, and so I'm just going to wait until they have a color that I really like, and then I'll go to town!

Day 246 – *Feeling of the Day*: Haunted

Oh no! No more plastic containers either!! I just watched a thing online about how bad plastic is for your body, and so plastic containers are not great. The BPA, which I've known about for a long time, actually leaches into your food. Not just when the plastic gets hot, but also in the cold. This bit was new to me. So, keeping your food in the plastic container in the fridge will still cause it to absorb the plastic and you're eating it!

And even if your containers are BPA-free, the industry has resorted to using another plastic softening agent, BSA (I forget what it stands for), which apparently is even worse than BPA. I haven't seen a single container marked as BPA and BSA-free!

So, I went to look for glass or even metal containers.

Almost all the glass containers I found still have plastic lids, no good! And of course, they are quite heavy, and the kids can't take them to school for their lunch!

So, I found stainless steel containers that are light and would work well for a lunch box. Only, they are expensive! Also, these still have plastic lids. Hmmm. The labels states 'BPA and lead-free'!

But I'm no dummy!! I suspect that the 'BPA-free' refers to the metal part of the container and not the lid. They would have still said the truth and yet been able to deceive the unsuspecting customer!!

See how twisted my mind has become? I simply assume the industry is out to get me! They are trying to use whatever is available and cheap, and don't care about manufacturing things that don't agree with my health!

Is this how I must live now?? I need to stop and breathe! Calm down! Nobody is out to get me! I just want some food containers. It's all good! I'll live for a while.

Oh, gotta go to yoga now, running late already!

Day 247 – *Feeling of the Day*: German

I went to buy a long board with Aaron today. He's been surfing for quite a while, but now he decided, it's time to have a board that he can use when there are next to no waves.

On the way back, we stopped by a small German shopping center. It's not close enough for me to go anytime I want, but this was a great opportunity to raid the butcher and the rest of the market! I bought up Bratwurst, Black Forest ham and other sausages. Loaded up on German rolls (for the boys' dinner only, of course), and red cabbage in the glass with apple sauce, one of my favorite vegetables. In fact, it's the first vegetable I ever liked (and I didn't like vegetables for a very, very long time when I was little)!

I also got some pickled sweet and sour red beets, as well as cabbage salad. My pantry looks very German right now, and I love it!!

No white asparagus in sight!

Day 248 – *Feeling of the Day*: Full of anticipation

This is it! I've sent THE email to Doc's office, asking if I should have my Big Day of Wheat any time soon. Let's see what he says!!

Four hours later:

No response yet. I'm waiting.

Meanwhile, I cooked a delicious lunch of lightly salted steamed cauliflower, and I pan-fried two of the terrific kale-veggie burgers that I found! I only burnt one side and was able to peel off one layer to reduce the two burgers to about one and one third of the originally planned meal.

But with lots of cauliflower, I felt pretty full until I realized that I totally forgot to include a protein! This is the original sin I committed over the years, and I am falling back into the trap. Essentially, I had veggies with veggies for lunch. Hmmm, sounds good to a certain extent. Just watch! I'll be hungry in about one hour!

20 minutes later:

I'm hungry! I need a snack! Maybe those bean crisps. They are surprisingly good and full of protein and salt. All the good stuff!

Day 249 – *Feeling of the Day*: Worried

Now I am starting to get kind of irritated. Doc responded in a short email to me that his recommendation is at least nine months.

What?!? Did I misunderstand?!? Or did he look at the wrong file??

I must clarify! This is not what I expected! It would mean another five months of gluten-free, so that makes it November. Still in time to eat Christmas Stollen during Christmas time! That is cutting it close!

Day 250 – *Feeling of the Day*: Getting prepared

Big relief! Doc had indeed thought that gluten was rated higher than one evil star for me, but now gave me the thumbs up for trying wheat when the time is right.

He gave me detailed instructions: I must be healthy and stable for about two weeks (got to get rid of this cough!!) and then have about three days of normal activity and normal stress level. Once I find this ideal window, I get to eat wheat in every meal for ONE day. Then: Note down what happens to me in every body system I can think of (or feel), to see if there's a negative impact for three days total.

Okay then!

Waiting for the time to be right. I feel as if I'm trying to get pregnant! So much waiting time, but it's critical to be juuuuuust right!

Day 251 – *Feeling of the Day*: Sigh...

A friend of mine told me that back in January, he got really sick with the flu as well, and it took him two months to get rid of that cough. That can't be good!

Day 252 – *Feeling of the Day*: Definitely not ready for this

It's officially beach season! School was out yesterday; this is the first day of summer break and I took the boys surfing this morning.

Right now, I feel as if I am always hungry, and I have no problem choosing a bunless burger over salad for lunch! Consequently, my belly is not looking so bikini-ish! ☹

We have a little over a week before heading out to Hawaii, better whip up some six-pack in that time. Worst case scenario, I'll have to spray-paint it on!

Day 254 – *Feeling of the Day*: Observing and learning

Since school is out, we've been to the beach every morning. I'm not looking any trimmer than two days ago. This worries me because our trip to Hawaii is now two days closer than before. Is it time for me to start wearing a one-piece bathing suit? In pursuit of kindness to others, it probably is.

Well, last night was hubby's 30th high school reunion, and indeed, I still must listen to my body! For late night dessert, I had to forego the cheesecake, although I really like cheesecake, and eat fruit instead. It was good, but again, this morning, my fingers felt a little more swollen and slower to regain their usual movement.

Alas, it's true! Food has a direct impact on your body, and I am learning to recognize the effects.

My next objective is to study what effect the three pieces of chocolate will have on my body that I ate at precisely 9pm. I'll be very attentive to my body for the next few hours before bedtime and again in the morning!

Day 256 – *Feeling of the Day*: Acknowledging the truth

Just five days before our summer vacation trip! There's no noticeable change in the tummy region, despite the walk I took this morning.

I know I have lost some weight while I was sick and been eating cautiously, but I realize that my 20-year old body is not coming back.

Bummer!!

Day 258 – *Feeling of the Day:* Too sensitive

I think I contaminated my own gluten-free tortillas! ☹ I was making dinner, Taco Thursday, because we had leftovers from the 30th high school reunion catering service. All I had to do was heat up lots of different parts of the meal, and I piled everything, the different meats, the tortillas, the beans etc. on various plates and heated things up in the microwave. Not the best, but it was getting late.

I put my GF tortillas on a plate and put the regular wheat tortillas on top, covered the plate with a paper towel and put it in the microwave.

I wasn't even thinking about contamination, I was focused on speed and practicality!

Hmmm! I didn't sleep well after that, tummy ache. ☹ I hope that's not a preview to my Big Day of Wheat!

Could have been the beans or the multitude of fruits I've been eating lately?

Day 259 – *Feeling of the Day*: Delayed

It seems that our time schedule has shifted to everything about 2 hours later than normal. It is summer break, so some leeway is okay, but now, it's affecting me! Our lunch was really good with Pasta Bolognese. The boys and I ate plentiful around 2pm.

Then coffee time at 5:30pm, and dinner didn't happen until 8pm. Since hubby made fried rice, I was going to have some of it, but then he added the spicy Korean sauce, which contains yeast extract, so that's a no-no for me.

I was left with leftover green salad with quinoa. That was not enough. Then I ate an apple, that wasn't enough either.

I finished off with the rest of my afternoon coffee, four oatmeal cookies. Small, but four, nevertheless.

Just splendid!

Now I'm finally full, of cookies and regrets!

Day 260 – *Feeling of the Day*: Dynamic

Garage Sale Day! All bets are off for breakfast! ☺

Well, I ate my rice bread with PBJ, just a bit later than usual – in-between selling my muffin pan and some plastic containers.

Made enough money to treat the fam and a friend to In-N-Out Burger for lunch. Oh no! It's bikini day in two days! That might not go over well.

Day 262 – *Feeling of the Day*: Heavenly

Bikini Day! We left for Maui this morning, already shopped for the basics to stock the pantry, and made it to our vacation rental. We dropped all the bags, just barely put the milk and eggs into the fridge and went straight into the ocean across the street.

Aaaaahhhhhh, bliss!!!

This is where I feel whole and peaceful!

Our family used to live here, four years in Hawaii total, 1½ years of those in Maui. Our good friend Gina came to see us later in the afternoon and said, "Welcome home!"

Tomorrow, I'll find the new big health food store that opened not too long ago to see if I can find pea milk! ☺

Day 263 – *Feeling of the Day*: Surprised and excited

I found pea milk!!!!! They really have it! I am stoked!! The same health food chain store near our home in CA doesn't carry it, so I wasn't expecting much. But here they do! I am so excited! ☺ Especially since I brought some cereal with me to Maui that I do not want to carry back home! It was just wishful thinking when I packed the cereal, and my wish came true! Pea milk on Maui! It can't get much better than this!

The only drawback is they don't have the regular or vanilla-flavored kind, only the unsweetened. It's a bit rough for cereal, but better than nothing. The other flavors are supposed to come in with a shipment expected for later in the afternoon.

Guess what? I'll be back here tomorrow!!

Day 264 – *Feeling of the Day*: Slightly disappointed

Guess what? Shipment was delayed because of a storm off the coast of Mexico. No vanilla-flavored pea milk! I bought the unsweetened kind, just so I have a breakfast alternative to my, oh, so exciting rice bread with peanut butter and jelly!

Shipment now expected for Friday. We'll see.

Day 266 – *Feeling of the Day*: Looking for sweetness

No chance to go back to the store yet. I'm living on unsweetened pea milk. Thank goodness, I have sweetened granola. I usually just mix the gluten-free oats with dried fruit to add to my cornflakes or other gluten-free cereal. During unsweetened times, however, granola is acceptable!

Day 267 – *Feeling of the Day*: Like eating children's food

I invented a new dish, and this is how it happened. Last night we drove up Haleakala, the massive volcano on Maui, to watch the sunset and see the stars. We used to do this at least once a month when we still lived here and still do it every time we come back to Maui. It makes for a beautiful drive, some awesome views and a picnic dinner in the back of the rented minivan, huddled in all the clothes we brought (it's very, very cold up there!)

On the way up, we stopped by the supermarket and grabbed something for dinner for everybody, except, I had brought my own food, which consisted of a gluten-free wrap, organic, grass-fed beef hot dog (need my protein!), and some fruit and chips (yes, chips – I'm on vacation!).

I also found a roasted veggie salad at the supermarket's deli counter. Happy me!

As I am setting out my food, I figured the easiest way to eating the various things was to roll the hot dog into the wrap and eat the veggies on the side. That's what I did. Then I looked up at Lucas who had picked a corn dog for dinner (he's on vacation, too!) I looked back at my roll and realized that I had created a grown-up, gluten-free version of a corn dog (sorta!).

Hmmm, that's how far I've come! I'm eating grown-up style corn dogs in the back of a minivan. Is this supposed to feel like progress?

I think not!

Day 268 – *Feeling of the* Day: Contemplating the future

Sushi lunch and down one pack of soy sauce! ☺

I lost count again so I might need to do the soy sauce piles again in the kitchen. I had also used a couple of packs during lunch with the in-laws shortly before leaving on vacation. So, there's been a near decimation of soy sauce in my stash. This is good.

I think that I have not gone below 170 packs yet. If I used roughly 30 packs in 9 months, then I will be covered for about 4½ more years! I expect the soy sauce pack consummation to be slowing down, simply because the beginning of this no-food year started with a greater enthusiasm for sushi than I had ever exhibited before. Then, there was also the incident in which I needed to open 14 packs to fill up a quarter cup for my Mongolian Beef crockpot recipe.

So, my calculation is vague if not completely off, and my stash might very well last me through the rest of my life. To infinity and beyond!!

I need to designate an heir to my soy stash. Someone who would appreciate the fact that this is gluten-free soy sauce! I will have to think carefully about whom I might choose. This is not a light-hearted decision!

Day 269 – *Feeling of the Day*: Freaked out

☹ No vanilla pea milk in sight! The shipment for the health food store has still not come in, and according to the helpful customer service person, the price tag has been removed from the shelf, which could mean one of two things, and both are bad:

1. The product is on backorder until further notice
2. The product has been discontinued

This better not be the case back in CA or I am going to DIE!!!

Day 270 – *Feeling of the Day*: Happy again

Happy Fourth of July to me!!! We went on a drive around the island, stopping by the viewpoints and small towns to browse, and what do I find??!! Vanilla pea milk in the health food store in Paia!! I am delighted and can move on with my vacation now!!

I happened to have a small cooler bag with me, so when we stopped for coffee after the health food store, I asked for two cups of ice to make sure my pea milk was going to make it through the rest of our tour.

I set the bag down on the ground while enjoying my Hawaiian coffee, but did not consider the fact that the cooler bag wasn't waterproof. The bag started leaking in the little coffee shop, so embarrassing!

Anyway, now that I have it, I haven't wasted another thought on how important pea milk is. Very superficial of me! Once a need is met, I move on to fulfilling the next.

What's my next need? I don't know. I will find out, I'm sure!

Oh yeah, slippahs! I need a new pair!

Day 272 – *Feeling of the Day*: Full of beef

Man, I've been eating burgers like there's no tomorrow! Fourth of July BBQ with the neighbors at our vacation rental in the evening, next day leftovers, today's beach and swimming pool day. Time to branch out and eat a grass-fed beef hot dog once in a while!

Day 273 – *Feeling of the Day*: Constipated

Salad, finally!! Today's dinner at a pizza place left me with very few choices, but, thank goodness, good choices they were! I had a family-size salad and shared with Rob only, adjusted the salad composition to have turkey, cheese, and olives removed (olives only because I'm not a fan, sorry!), and there you have it!

I've been experiencing this thing where digestion is slow, and things aren't moving along, and it takes a long time when in the bathroom. Fine! I'm constipated and it's not fun! Especially, when I spend most my daytime at some beach and I must sit on the beach park restroom toilet rather than in the comfort of my own home.

Why though? I've been avoiding rice again as much as possible (except for when it's the main flour used in my bread, the GF wrap or in my cookies). Hopefully, tonight's salad was a bit of help.

After dinner, we went to one of the fancy shopping centers nearby with an even fancier ice cream shop – Lappert's!!! The only way to eat ice cream on the island, unless you buy Roselani ice cream at the local supermarket!

Anyway, I went into the little store just to be with Aaron and Lucas, watching them pick their favorite flavor, knowing that I couldn't have any.

And then I saw it – Sorbets in island flavors! Dairy-free! Looked good!!! I got a taste of the Luau Delight flavor (lilikoi and coconut), and it was DELICIOUS!!! I had bought ice cream made from coconut milk back at home from the health food store, and it was good at first, but the more I tasted it, the less I liked it. No good, plus the flavors always seem to be the same: Peanut butter, chocolate, peanut butter, more peanut butter.

Lilikoi and coconut was different!!! It was so good! I can't wait to go back!

Yay, ice cream on my vacation! ☺ Oh, shucks! Vacation-related weight gain. Oh dear! ☹

Day 274 – *Feeling of the Day*: Stable

I am mentally preparing for my Big Day of Wheat. I know Doc had said I needed two weeks of stability. I am feeling very stable these days, and my cough is long gone.

After those two weeks, I will need three days of normal, moderate stress only. I will time it so that the Big Day of Wheat falls into the time period when we are back home. I think it'll be easier to control the foods during my regular home routine.

Waiting!

Day 275 – *Feeling of the Day*: Maybe unstable?

Does constipation mess with my 'period of stability'? If so, I'm not in a stable place yet.

Producing pebbles!!

Day 277 – *Feeling of the Day*: Overheated

Oh no, I woke up with fingers feeling slightly swollen! Wondering if I've been having too much meat? Or is it from the heat? Hawaii weather at its finest! ;)

Day 278 – *Feeling of the Day*: Ignorant

Woke up this morning; fingers are fine. Must have been the heat.

Last night I had an interesting conversation with a lady who has been a vegetarian for several years and I learned a lot. For example, the fact that meat contains uric acid that can cause arthritis, so maybe I shouldn't rely on meat so much for my protein. Haven't had fish in a while, only once during our vacation so far.

Also, she told me that Africa produces enough rice and wheat to feed its population; however, the grains are being shipped to Europe as food for cattle because this brings in more money for the farm owners. What a shame! I really didn't know this before.

Day 279 – *Feeling of the Day*: Taking a mishap in stride

Unknowingly, I seriously violated my diet today. Hubby prepared Kalbi, the Korean BBQ beef, and it was delicious!! The meat was pre-packaged and marinated in Teriyaki sauce. Later, I found that packaging and to my horror, I read wheat AND yeast extract in the list of ingredients! ☹

I know, I'll be paying for this tomorrow. Watch my fingers feel swollen again in the am.

Nevertheless, I did not let myself be devastated by this misstep. Happily, I went back to Lappert's Ice Cream to have coconut milk sorbet. I might need to move in there!

Day 280 – *Feeling of the Day*: Disorganized

I feel fat today! All throughout the vacation, I've been keeping in decent shape. The fact that I put on a bathing suit every single day helps with the self-control as far as Maui Potato Chips are concerned. Also, I've been swimming or paddle boarding every day, so there's a workout.

Today, however, we took the boys to a beach, which is predominantly a surfing beach. There are rocks and corals too close to the shore, so that it's not really a swimmable beach. We met with a friend and her grandson who played with Aaron and Lucas, while the adults stayed on the grassy area overlooking the small tide pool for the very young, and never got up to get in the water.

Today was the first day I did not get into the ocean at all. Nevertheless, I ate heartily and enjoyed my GF cookies with the best coffee, Maui Mocha, in the afternoon. Then, we stopped by the island's newest skate park for Aaron one last time, and by the time we got home, it was 9pm.

I just had my dinner!

So, here is how I've been falling off the diet plan. I've been having dinners way late (regardless of whether I look at California time or Hawaii time). I've had fresh fruit in the evenings; I've had a few non-organic burgers (aka pink slime from the bulk pack) and lots of them; and finally, no fish except once during these three weeks. No potatoes either.

Tomorrow is our last full day, and we will be eating our leftovers of a couple of burger patties, an orange, two mangos and a peach, cereal, one of my single portion package of lentil soup, lots of rice and one six pack of Aloha drinks (for the boys). Should be interesting! ☺

Oh yeah, about the burgers. I had bought a small pack of organic, grass-fed beef burger patties and cooked one for myself the other day. Then, I cooked two patties of the other, non-organic kind and watched them shrink to about two thirds of their size in frozen state.

Very, very weird! Why would they shrink so much?

The organic one didn't! Is that a sign of one being real food and the other not so much?

Puzzling.

Day 281 – *Feeling of the Day*: Enjoying my last opportunity for sorbet

Lilikoi and coconut sorbet, AGAIN, at the gelato place! I need to move here!!!

Day 282 – *Feeling of the Day:* **Down**

Aloha Hawaii! Leaving today. ☹

Pebbles . . .

Day 283 – *Feeling of the Day*: Making up for lost veggies

We arrived home just before midnight last night. I just woke up and the most exciting part of the day so far has been to step on the scale and see what lilikoi-coconut sorbet does to my mid-section.

Adds about one pound!

Good thing I didn't discover the sorbets until late into our vacation or else!! Three weeks of sorbet wouldn't have been so favorable. Of course, this could be muscle mass as well, from all that paddling and frolicking in the water. Although strangely, all muscles got added around the hips and the belly. I must have had some lack there?!?

Here is today's mission – Since our fridge is empty (except for the PB&J sandwiches that nobody ate on the flight), I'll be grocery shopping after unpacking the bunch.

There'll be lots of fresh fruit (which I was NOT lacking in Hawaii!!) and lots of vegetables (uh, slightly neglected ☹). There won't be any hot dogs or burgers for me for a while.

Hmmm, what can I eat?!? It's been so long, I already forgot!

On the other hand, I can't be overbuying stuff because we're leaving for Korea in ten days to a wedding!! Since the flight is super long, 13 hours (!), we're also staying for ten days to make it worthwhile! Aaron and Lucas have never been to Korea although Rob still has family there, so they need to get a good look at their other half of ancestry this time.

Today's motto is to get groceries but buy with good measure only!

Day 285 – *Feeling of the Day*: Pleasantly surprised

The 9pm dinners continue! I don't know what time zone I'm supposed to be in. I think I'm in Spain! Sounds about right with the long siesta after lunch and late-night dinner.

Well, today is my father-in-law's 80th birthday, and we went out to a very fancy Korean restaurant – a rehearsal for next week and the following ten days of Korean food. I think I'm going to gain much more muscle mass then! ;)

I also think I'm going to have to push my Big Day of Wheat past all this travel, i.e. after Korea. I guess, the most stable time period will occur when I'm back home with my regular foods for a couple of weeks. That puts the Big Day of Wheat into late August. Maybe, I'll just make it my birthday, the 31st.

On another note, I went to the mall today and checked the sorbets at the gelato stand. Don't you know it! They had coconut-passionfruit sorbet!!!! How come I never saw this before? So, it's not a Hawaii special? Where have I been?

Hiding in my no-food misery is where I've been, not seeing the decadent foods that are all around me and allowed.

Huh! I need to get out more! ☺

Day 286 – *Feeling of the Day*: Concerned

After the fancy late dinner last night, I am still feeling full. I had fish and veggies and only had very little rice because that constipation situation has not yet disappeared completely.

So now I wonder, what's going to happen when we are in Korea for ten days with daily rice? Will I ever be able to go to the bathroom again? Or will I just blow up like a balloon?

Hmmm.

Day 287 – *Feeling of the Day*: I want a redo of this day

Oh man, what a day!!! Hubby came home all grumpy today after a rough week at work. I'm sure it's not been easy going back after such a nice vacation, but today was especially hard. Then, Lucas got mad because he had to read while Aaron got to run out and visit with the neighbors. And right before bedtime, Aaron got impatient with me because I didn't know what an EA-account is. Apparently, it's an account that needs to be set up for certain video games, but since I don't play games at all, I have no clue. Despite his efforts to try and make me understand, it didn't click.

Yikes!! Everybody is angry around me!! I am feeling a secondhand anger and uncontrolled potato-chip-eating session coming my way!

Twenty minutes later:

Angry potato-chip-eating session happened, topped off with a piece of dark chocolate AND I'm watching old political thriller TV shows!

Can I scratch this day off the calendar?

Day 289 – *Feeling of the Day*: Frightened

Two scary things happened today. One was cauliflower crust pizza, topped with broccoli, and the other was the fact that the cookie sheet I had just bought brand-new, popped very loudly inside the oven while baking said pizza and was all curved after that.

I found the pizza crust at my local market and it seemed like a good idea then, but today, after we decided to eat all stuff out of the freezer, I pulled it out and figured, I needed to top it with lots of good stuff.

Unfortunately, I have no ready-to-eat protein on hand right now (ham, hot dog or other) that would enhance the flavor. Instead, I had frozen broccoli, some fresh mushrooms and zucchini. I put all of that on the pizza, but first, there must be tomato sauce, right?!?!

Given the fact that we are leaving again in three days, I didn't want to open a tomato sauce jar, so I reached for salsa instead. The only salsa I had was my mild peach salsa. Turns out, peach and broccoli don't go together so well.

Everybody at the table was super scared of my pizza. Only hubby was brave enough to try and had tears in his eyes when he chewed the thing. Well, that was lunch! ☺

I have to say, it did look really good. If only there had been proper tomato sauce, some meat and some cheese, I think, this could be really something! (For later when I'm allowed those things again. Maybe.)

The cookie sheet incident turned out to be of minor importance. I had bought two trays a few weeks ago, and this was not the first time I used it. The non-stick cookie trays are aluminized steel bakeware made with titanium and ceramic. That's what it says, and they are PTFE/ PROA/and PFOS free. All bad things, but I forgot what they all stand for. I just feel good knowing that these things are not in my food!

In any case, after cooling off, the cookie sheet returned to its original form and we're all good.

Now, I need some ice cream to offset the extreme lunch!

Day 291 – *Feeling of the Day*: Relieved

I finally figured it out! I remembered what I used to do with the boys when they were little and having a hard time with the 'Going to the bathroom, number two' situation.

Two words: Prune juice!!

I got a bottle and I have been drinking a glass each day since the day before yesterday. Thank goodness!! I mean it was getting ugly!! After last night's dinner, I felt so stuffed, as if the food was filling my belly up to my neck, and my stomach was out of control! Unreal!!

Finally, this morning, there was relief and I felt as if I was back to being myself! Just myself!!☺

So, prune juice might be a new item in the fridge every now and then. It took a little over a day to really take effect, but all natural and tasty, if in a weird way

Still, I can't figure out though, what caused the slow-mo!

Day 292 – *Feeling of the Day*: Eager to find out how this will turn out

Going to Korea Day! We are leaving the house after lunch. Our flight leaves at 6pm. This is a 13-hour trip! Yikes!!! Don't know what to expect, but it'll be a new adventure!

The boys are having mixed feelings, mainly because "Where is there a skate park?" (Aaron!) and "What is there to do anyways?" (Lucas!). Hmmm. I have been looking at the top ten things to do in Seoul and found several things that looked interesting (mostly for grown-ups), so we shall see.

My suitcase contains my very nice dress, fancy shoes, etc. for the wedding on Saturday. Then some more clothes and then lots of food (snacks, gluten-free cereal, cookies, one pack of pasta, etc.). I'll see how this is going.

I'm also bringing my fake, vegan creamer although I know they have fancy coffee shops over there. But you never know. Besides, I don't like to have soy creamer every day. The fake creamer has been okay, depending on the coffee (although I am really convinced that it is just canola oil with white paint in it.).

Well, that's still dairy-free! ☺

Okay, leaving the house in 5,4,3,2,1! SCARY!!!

Later in the airplane:

Here we go: Nutritional freefall II – on my way to Korea!!

It might not be a good start since I am still dealing with some constipation. No success in the bathroom yesterday or today. Well, I don't really want to block the airplane bathroom for ½ hour just trying to go during the flight. So, I'm doing everyone a favor and am staying away!

Day 293 – *Feeling of the Day*: Reassured

My pre-ordered gluten-free meal on the airplane was chicken! So, I gave it to hubby and took his Korean beef from the regular meal! The veggies were delicious, and I couldn't help but eat some rice because it was all so tasty! A wonderful prospect of things to come!

Day 294 – *Feeling of the Day*: Finding ways to make do

We're in our tiny studio hotel room all unpacked and already had breakfast. The website for our hotel had shown a toaster in our room, so I brought some rice bread and buckwheat waffles.

There's no toaster, so I pan-fried my waffle, no oil (because there is none)! Will hit the Korean supermarket later today and figure out what there is. ☺

End of the day:

Ok, so we never made it to the supermarket, but instead started walking the streets. Just barely venturing out of the hotel in Gangnam district when Rob's cousin (2nd degree) came to take us around town and to lunch AND dinner. OMG, the food is a problem, not because of my restrictions, but because it's so very good and plentiful! An amazing number of choices for me, too!

I think I'll be happy and fat in Korea!

So, our lunch consisted of a traditional Korean BBQ beef and veggies, including many varieties of kimchee (the spicy fermented cabbage). It was yummy. No health food store required, and even the kids ate up!

For dinner, we went to an Italian place since hubby's cousin (cuz) wanted to change things up a bit.

I had a salad and I really wish I knew what was in there! It was extremely tasty and would be something I'd like to try and imitate.

Cuz's niece, who met us for dinner, spoke good English and helped translate the menu. I asked her about the salads. She told me that the one I was interested in included mushrooms, feta cheese and slices of beef steak. I told her I'd like it only without the cheese. Then the waiter came, and I asked him also what was in that salad. He said quinoa and red wine vinegar. I asked if it had mixed greens, leafy veggies and he said "yes".

When he served the salad there were no green leaves. In fact, it was more of a stir fry than salad and I couldn't make out what else could have been in there. (It was kind of dark in the restaurant; I was tired; my eyes are going bad – all the above!). I gobbled it up anyway! Yummy!!

On another note, I woke up and one of my molars hurt, but when I went to brush my teeth, I found that it was actually the gum that was swollen and sensitive. Dang it!! I had totally forgotten about the gum inflammations that I had coming around.

Wasn't the last one when I was in Germany? It was a short-lived one if I remember correctly.

In any case, it's annoying that it's still popping up. Well, hopefully not for long!

I finally was able to go the bathroom a little, too. Yesterday, a thought occurred to me. Maybe it's the number of supplements that's causing at least part of the constipation?

Gee! Can't do a thing right!

Exhausted from a whole day of sightseeing in Seoul, I'm going to sleep now. Tomorrow is the big day, other cuz's wedding!

Good night for now!

Day 295 – *Feeling of the Day*: Mixed with various emotions

I bought juicy plums from the tiny market around the corner to get my digestion moving. I had three in one day and therefore a small success on the loo. ☺

Now, if I could only stop eating rice with the meals. I'm keeping it down low, but impossible to go without it completely.

Also, my gum still hurts when brushing teeth, the infection spread upwards. I am not happy about that! Everything else is okay. When we get back home, I'll have to go back to a stricter diet as in organic foods, grass-fed beef, etc. Who knows which of the meats are marinated (and in what?) and what's in those sauces anyway?

This makes it really difficult to monitor everything!

We're getting ready to go to cuz's wedding in a little while (the reason for this entire trip!) I'm VERY curious to see it. I know some of the family members that will be there. As for all the other wedding guests who are non-English-speaking persons (which means almost everybody else), there'll be happy smiling and consistent nodding on my part.

Day 296 – *Feeling of the Day:* Overwhelmed

The day after. OMG, the wedding!!! One of those affairs where everything is planned out to the 'T' and 250 people easily get shuffled around from the ceremony to the banquet hall back to the picture op with precision and ease!

It was phenomenal! Cuz was too cute, so very happy and handsome! Lucas said he thought the bride was very beautiful, but she didn't seem to resemble her parents much. I don't quite know how to interpret that. I'm just gonna be happy he thought she was beautiful, and indeed she was!

The wedding included the Western-style church ceremony with a pre-recorded video message from each the bride and groom to each of their respective in-laws and then their own parents as well. Seeing the strong emotions on their faces while expressing their love and gratitude in the video made me cry even though I didn't understand a single word (because it was in Korean of course!)

The food was buffet style with a large dining area, free choice of seats, somewhat like the Las Vegas-style buffet restaurants. The buffet included a large variety of Korean foods, but also Italian foods, sushi and more. No lack of choices (or restraint in serving sizes)!

After everything was said and done, late afternoon, we parted. In fact, we were kind of ushered out of the banquet hall as the next wedding party was trickling in. We went back to our hotel to change and rest briefly just to go out yet again for one of the millions of coffee shops in our area.

I think if Koreans are over making smartphones, cars, and TVs, they can start exporting coffee shop ideas! This seems to be one of the major trends in the Gangnam district. At night, we descended into the small and narrow streets behind the large boulevards. Plastered with shrill and colorful neon signs, these streets are filled with food stands, small restaurants, markets and tiny shops where nobody knows what they're really selling.

Since the boys were pretty much done with all the walking and eating, we just picked up food from the street vendors and took it back to our place.

Two out of four selections were okay. But, no problem; tomorrow is another restaurant — uh, day!

Day 298 – *Feeling of the Day*: Overcome by sesame seeds

Aaron is constipated! I bought lots more fruit so that the whole family can be 'productive'!

I noticed that this country has an entire surplus of sesame seeds! They're EVERYWHERE!!! Since I'm not supposed to eat seeds, it's been time-consuming to pick around, but that should help keep my waist small (Haha!). We went to a restaurant that is known for its fabulous kimchee, but each single selection was sprinkled with sesame seeds!

One of my favorite dishes, glassy-looking noodles (made of sweet potatoes) mixed with strips of beef, bell peppers, mushrooms, chives etc., is typically infused with sesame seeds plus sesame seed sprinkles on top.

Yesterday, one of the uncles invited us to breakfast. He took us to a traditional place in the business district of Seoul. We had beef broth with beef slices, mixed with rice again – for breakfast! And it was sprinkled with sesame seeds on top!

Stop it already! Show some sympathy for the seed-sensitive people like me, pleeeeeeeeeease!!! It's so hard stripping the seeds off each glass noodle! Now I understand how life in Korea can have its downsides.

Maybe I'm the only person in the world with a seed issue? Hmmm.

Day 299 – *Feeling of the Day*: Shocked to the core

So yesterday, I ate something that I really don't know if I even want to write about it. It was because of the boys. They had planned on trying this out long before we even got on the plane; I never was inclined to partake in this.

Last night, one of hubby's friends picked us up from this busy, lively student quarter of the city and drove us to a rather obscure part of the city. Really, I don't even know if it was still part of the city; the streets became lonelier and lonelier. It was near the harbor and looked like there was nothing but abandoned storage halls from long-gone industry. And there, just before a tunnel that led straight out of town (maybe even straight into North Korea?!?), were a few small buildings and one little neon sign lit up, indicating that there was someone alive in this remote area. Oddly enough, some new and very fancy cars were parked in front of that little building.

We got out of the car, entered the little place, and were led into a backroom that had already been prepared for us. The table down low had been set up with all the little bowls of side dishes, and two individual hot plates with gas burners were at the ready for the main courses to be served.

We took off our shoes, entered the room and sat cross-legged in front of the tables. It felt most unreal! But I couldn't get out; there was nowhere else to go!

The waitress arrived with one of the main dishes that was a whole chicken in its broth and covered with leafy green veggies. This was obviously for Rob and his friend, since he didn't want to eat the other dish to come.

And then the main, main dish arrived! A large bowl filled with meat in its own broth, layered with chives and other greens stewing before my very eyes.

The boys admitted that they were nervous to eat. Since this had been their doing, they had no choice but to help themselves and eat up. They did!

They said it just tasted like meat and nothing different. They started telling me I should try, but I was hesitant. I just couldn't. But they were so insistent, and I thought of all the times I had told Aaron to just try that piece of broccoli/cauliflower/mushroom/you-name-it. How could I refuse? Not modeling what I ask of them??

So, I picked the smallest piece of meat I could possibly find in the stew — size of my thumbnail — added some greens and stared at it . . . for a long time!

I kept blowing on it, pretending it was still too hot to eat. But everybody at the table looked at me, waiting to see me eat it. I brought the meat close to my face, looked at it some more, and suddenly, I cried!

Tears were welling up; it was ridiculous!! I don't know where that came from, but Lucas who was sitting next to me comforted me and said: "It's okay, Mom, it's just meat and it's already dead anyways."

I was so embarrassed to be so dramatic! That had not been my intention at all! I started laughing and finally, still looking at this tiny, tiny piece of meat at the tip of my chopsticks, Aaron gave me a countdown to put it in my mouth: "3, 2, 1!"

And there you have it! I ate DOG!!

It tasted just like seasoned meat, like game.

After that one single bite, I put my chopsticks down and didn't eat anything else until we got home. All I could think of were the cute dogs that I personally know. My neighbor's and friends' pets, etc.

I felt terrible towards Rob's friend who had treated us to this special and very expensive dinner. I apologized to him profusely, trying to tell him that I had no idea I was going to feel this strongly about it when the time came. He was very nice about it and I hope he'll forgive me for the drama.

Usually, I'm not one to make a big fuss, especially in public, but this one was special!

I can't believe I ate it!

Day 300 – *Feeling of the Day*: Lost in translation

We are nearing the end of our stay in Korea. Foodwise, I could totally live here, although my body shape seems to change for the unfavorable. I'd like to be more voluminous on the top and skinny around the belly. However, the reverse is reality.

And with the Korean diet, heavy on meat (lots of pork, including heavy pork belly) and all this rice, it might not be the best for me in the long run.

Actually, it seems that being in Korea majorly revolves around food. We met a lot of family members I hadn't met before, and every single meeting was either for lunch or dinner plus coffee time. We'd get together to go to specific restaurants that are famous for one kind of food or another. On a couple of occasions, more people showed up that I didn't know, and mysteriously, they are all related to hubby somehow. Everybody is somehow either 'uncle' or 'cousin'.

There was a young man that joined us for lunch yesterday and Rob just mentioned that he is yet another cousin. I looked at Rob, puzzled, because I was pretty sure I knew all the actual first-degree cousins. Rob explained: "You know, my mother's mother, her cousin's daughter's son!" ☺

Ahh!! Got it!!

Lucas asked me: "Sooo, who is that?" Throwing my hands up in the air, I responded: "For you, Uncle!"

Then I asked Rob what cousin's name was. Rob thought about it for a moment and admitted that he didn't know. But that is not necessarily unusual because Korean's call each other by title rather than name, titles as in 'older brother', 'aunt from my mother's side' and such. I'm so lost as to what to call anybody, I just smile and nod. ☺

When I asked Rob and his (real) cousin (the groom) how I should address the bride, a five-minute discussion ensued between the two. It's not easy! I'm the wife of the groom's older cousin on his mother's side. I am also older than the bride, which needs to be considered. The two of them finally agreed on a title that I couldn't pronounce.

I smile and nod. ☺

Day 301 – *Feeling of the Day*: Thankful for air conditioning

Today, we're expecting a high of 94 degrees Fahrenheit and 76% humidity. That's down from almost 85% humidity a couple of days ago. Nevertheless, because of the temperature, today is the 'National Museum of Korea to see Asian arts' day. That should be nice! We've already seen two large and beautiful palaces and different parts of the city with well-preserved traditional houses. Sooo incredibly picturesque!

Wandering around the palace in all these little pathways and through the gates makes me imagine what life may have been like hundreds of years ago! Only without A/C or iced coffee.

Lucky us! We'll be going off in the metro with modern A/C, into the museum with giant A/C and then to the restaurant with hyper-A/C. Better bring a jacket.

Day 302 – *Feeling of the Day*: So satisfied with the food

Our last day in Korea! ☹ Same morning routine as the previous few days – light breakfast in our hotel room (my hand-carried waffle or cereal with pea milk), then get picked up by cousin and go to lunch with an insane number of bowls full of various types of kimchee and other veggies. Plus the meat in a stew or BBQ style. Plus sesame seeds.

Today, however, we didn't do any further sightseeing because of 96 degrees Fahrenheit, so we went to 'Auntie's' home, a condo outside of Seoul where we had coffee and played with her three dogs until late afternoon.

Aaron and Lucas want a dog now (not to eat)!

Since the food was so agreeable to my diet, I am now left with an insane number of snacks that I had brought with me, just in case. This is kind of ridiculous, but oh well, better safe than sorry!

We finished off our fabulous Korea visit as we went out to see a light show at Gangnam Square after dark and hiked back up to our hotel one last time in the still hot and muggy air.

Tomorrow we leave! Due to the time difference, we will arrive back in Los Angeles before we leave Seoul!

"Ha!" I told Aaron and Lucas, "Try and figure out that one!"

Day 303 – *Feeling of the Day*: Annoyed with hair loss

Today I am taking my new-found Korean-food-belly home on an 11+ hours flight. We'll see what my scale at home has to say about that.

One of my longest minor (but annoying) ailments has been an annual bout of hair loss during summer. This has been happening for several years now, and believe me, it's been an event! So, I've been watching this summer's hair situation and I'm not entirely convinced that it's <u>not</u> happening. Even though I'd been taking vitamin Bs, specifically biotin for the hair, it never really helped because of lack of protein. I never absorbed the vitamins, which is why I'm now trying to get protein with each meal!

This morning I felt as if there was more hair collecting down in the drain than should have been. Man!! This is so not wanted!!

It looks as if I am shedding my winter fur!

And what other causes are there for hair loss? I know it could be tons of things, one of them being stress. And hair loss often occurs 3 months after a major stress event.

So, what happened 3 months ago?? I don't know! I was probably expecting summer to happen and stressing over potential hair loss!

Later in the day, in the airplane:

6 hours and 30 minutes to go! All the fruit we've been eating worked – for Aaron!

As for me, meh, well, I can go, but it's not all that gratifying.

During our time in Korea, I had minimal salad and plenty of foods unusual to my body. After all, Aaron is half-Korean and probably processing rice much better than I am?

My personal ancestry processes potatoes and Schnitzel quite well. So, let me go back to that and more fruit, and then let's see what happens.

Day 304 – *Feeling of the Day*: Relieved

Back at home:

Yay, plums are working!!

Day 305 – *Feeling of the Day*: Wooowwwwww, more relief than I could have imagined

OMG! Are they ever working!!!!! Plums and all the other fruit! I think I need to eat some rice tonight.

If I had a behavior chart for my organs, my digestive system would get a gold star today! Fully back in the swing of all things digestion. That's all I have to say about that!

Day 306 – *Feeling of the Day*: Sleepless and headachy

My hair loss is definitely up; I am sure now. It's more than I like! And last night, I came down with a headache again, totally unprovoked!! I took half a pill and then had to deal with Lucas, who came back out of his bedroom after midnight, unable to sleep because of jetlag and having sweat in his bed. I found myself changing his sheets in the middle of the night with a headache, sent the boy to take a shower to cool off, and then he asked to sleep in my bed.

Hubby was already in bed, so the two of us (Lucas and me) crammed in next to hubby, who eventually fell down on the floor and slept there.

My headache never went away; I hardly slept because of it. Then it stayed throughout the whole day despite another half pill this morning.

I ran some errands, including doing a return at the mall today when I remembered that I had seen the fabulous sorbet at the gelato place AND I remembered someone telling me that ice cream is good for headaches! So, my master plan is to eat ice cream/sorbet and rid myself of the headache!

Well, they didn't have the wonderful coconut-passionfruit flavor that I thought I had seen there a few weeks ago, only lemon or raspberry. The raspberry was too sweet, so I ended up eating a full serving of lemon sorbet which just about sucked my entire face together with its acidity!!

After a few more errands, I made it home, took an hour nap, had some coffee, and, at last, when the air finally cooled down late afternoon, the headache went away while I was watching Lucas's soccer practice. I must say, this is the first time the headache simply disappeared during the day without another pain pill. Usually, I must sleep it off overnight. So, this is not bad, but the headache itself is really not good either.

Neutral – at best!

Day 307 – *Feeling of the Day*: Floored

Feeling a little off these days. Partially because of jetlag, of course, but I am now convinced that all this eating out over 10 days in Korea might not have been the best, simply because I cannot control 100% of what I eat.

My conclusion is that I most likely ate more things I shouldn't have, and this is how I, Sherlock Holmes, have cleverly come to this conclusion:

I had lunch at our boys' favorite burger restaurant, and with all my tweaking of their menu, I had still enjoyed my meals there previously. Today, I went in and ordered grilled fish tacos on corn tortillas, and I even remembered to ask for the sauce on the side and no cheese.

Then I said, "Actually, no dairy at all."

The friendly waiter replied: "Oh, in that case, I'll ask them to not put butter on the tortillas before stuffing them!"

Wait, what?!??? @#$%$@%#$%#@#%$(%^#

You mean, I've been trying all this time (btw, I am now at 10 months, TEN MONTHS!!!!), and I am STILL not eating clean enough food??? How much longer can I mess up before I get it?!?

WUAAAAAAHHHHHHH!

Day 308 – *Feeling of the Day*: Getting angry

Ah! I just speed-read yet another book about nutrition, which came highly recommended from two of my friends independently of each other. This book explains how the different blood types evolved in the various ancestries of the world and how they each process food differently, some better than others, depending on your type. It makes sense when I read it, so this would become the life-long ideal diet to follow for optimal health.

I am blood type O and, in addition to Doc's restriction list, can now, according to the book, no longer eat pork (including ham or bacon), not a single type of cheese ever again, coconut or safflower oil, peanuts or peanut butter, kidney or navy beans or any type of lentils, cornflakes, any bread ever, including pumpernickel (Hello, I'm German!!!), spinach pasta or soba noodles (although buckwheat is allowed, hmmm).

These are all baffling because with my new diet, I've eaten more pork, and, of course, peanuts/peanut butter, lentils and beans in order to get protein!! And coconut oil and cornflakes have become new staples due to cutting out all the other good stuff!

But here's the real killer!

In the department of vegetables, the book says for me to avoid: Avocado, any type of cabbage (have been eating kimchee for the past ten days and more!!!), cauliflower (the only cruciferous veggie that I really like. Wince!), corn, eggplant, mushrooms (I eat often), as well as red or white potatoes.

I'm asking you: If I must take it easy on rice due to constipation risk, and cannot have pasta, where else is my mass going to come from? Potatoes!!! But NO, cannot!

And fruit? Guess what? No more blackberries, coconut, cantaloupe or honeydew melon, oranges (ORANGES!!!) and strawberries!!!

I am crying! ☹

Then I looked up hubby's 'Avoid List', him being a Korean blood type B and all. His list had: Coconuts, persimmons, pomegranates, prickly pear, rhubarb and starfruit!

Seriously? How hard is it to cut out persimmon and prickly pear?!?!! Rhubarb?!?? Who even knows what that looks like?!????

How come he always gets the easy part of the deal?? Now, I'm not crying! Now, I'm angry!!

It's past midnight, but I'm just going to get my computer and watch some mean show! So there!! ☹☹

Day 309 – *Feeling of the Day*: Trying to calm myself

Ok, slow down! I might have overreacted yesterday. I'm simply going to send an email to Doc, asking his opinion about the above. And then, I can react again. After all, he tested my very specific own blood reactions to all these foods.

Maybe, I have evolved enough to tolerate avocado and oranges? (I'm crossing my fingers for those two and potatoes, cauliflower and mushrooms) And kimchee and corn, oh, and peanuts!! Of course, lentils and beans!

Otherwise, I see my sources of protein shrinking to next to nothing! I don't even know anymore! I mean, how many times a day/week can I eat beef and buffalo?!?

Ok, stop hyperventilating and start emailing! Here we go!

Day 310 – *Feeling of the Day*: Really, really frustrated

I am so frustrated, it's not even funny! I haven't started writing the email to Doc yet, but it's gonna be a long one.

We just watched a video tutorial on how to make chap chae, a Korean noodle dish (mixed with vegetables and BBQ beef), one of my favorites. And low and behold, it contains soy sauce! I thought it only had sesame oil in it, and I thought I had read the list of ingredients carefully when we bought some at the Korean supermarket. Of course, any meat or other dishes that are prepared with soy sauce at that market or in Korea itself won't be prepared with gluten-free soy sauce.

So, for 10 days in Korea, I've been eating many foods with regular soy sauce – especially the meats.

I am so depressed! I feel like I can't win! Things keep popping up that I didn't know about. I feel so ignorant; everything seems to be going backwards.

It is looking more and more that I need to prepare ALL my foods at home and can never go back out and eat something off the shelf or in a restaurant, or I'm just gonna die because I'm not a great cook! I think, I mentioned that before.

I am so frustrated!!!!! How can I be so dumb? ☹

But the physical effects I've been feeling recently include that pesky constipation, increased loss of hair, and three days of a nagging headache. Each of those disappeared over the course of the day, but they were still unpleasant.

So maybe, I won't need my Big Day of Wheat after all. The results are already in and they're not good!

I still need to email Doc with my questions. Maybe later. For now, I'll just dwell in my frustration for a little while.

Day 312 – *Feeling of the Day*: Hectic

I finally got around to writing that email to Doc. Since he's typically a man of two-word-responses, I hope he won't be overwhelmed by my long email, addressing about four issues at once. I tend to be wordy. (I can just see him read these notes one day and go, "No sh*t!!")

Waiting for a lot of verdicts.

In the meantime, my time is running out. I have to catch up on my admin work, and my accounting work. I picked up a new client roughly 40 miles from here, a lovely lady, but the appointments take the better part of my afternoon (really, all of it), and my Mom arrives in two days for a four-week stay!

I am really looking forward to my Mom's visit, but I wanted to get so many things done before then.

Anyhow, I'm off to pick up Aaron from his high school freshman orientation, then lunch, and then going to my afternoon work appointment!

Busy day!

Day 314 – *Feeling of the Day*: Full of self-pity

Doc definitely got overwhelmed with my email! He has neither responded nor acknowledged it. Or could he be on vacation?

But the excessive hair loss is real! I am weirded out! What would cause this in the middle of the year of getting healthy?!? Severe pouting continues! ☹

Day 317 – *Feeling of the Day*: Troubled

Fright is setting in! I can't even count the number of hairs I am losing. I bought a Restore-and-Strengthen shampoo and conditioner, my hairdresser recommended taking biotin and a vitamin B complex (which I am already doing) and massaging my scalp to stimulate blood circulation.

That's all good, except that the massaging makes my hair look like a bird's nest. At least, there are a few twigs left!

I'm not happy. ☹

Day 319 – *Feeling of the Day*: Hypothesizing

Gee, I think if my life was ever turned into a movie, the lead actress would have to be Drew Barrymore. Made in the way of *50 First Dates* about a normal, nice woman with bad things happening to her (for a while).

But then I think about her role in *Charlie's Angels,* which means she's also kind of badass. That's not me!

Scratch that thought.

Day 320 – *Feeling of the Day*: Suffering again

Doc is no longer MIA! He got lost in Berlin, Germany. Needless to say, I can't go see him. He was also not able to answer all my questions via text :(

I've been massaging my head for the last few days (hoping for hair regrowth), thinking that things will eventually just return to normal, as they have each of the last few years. However, each of those years, I ended up cutting my hair just a little shorter because the ends looked too thinned out then. If that continues, I will soon have a buzz cut!

Also, I am still eating plums, just because I bought too many. In addition, I bought cherries and berries, and now have way too much fruit in the house. Cherries are nearly overripe now, just borderline, and boy, did things speed up in the bathroom!

Lastly, a small headache started up AGAIN yesterday late afternoon (on my way home from a client visit). It continued throughout the night and I woke up with it again this morning. Same thing the night before. Each night was too short, so I finally figured out what caused the headaches – it's the dang clock!!! I wake up, look at the time, and there's the headache! So, if I didn't have the time, maybe no headache?!?

It's 1:23am; I've been naughty and watched TV shows until just a few minutes ago. Let's see if that clock gives me a headache tomorrow! If I wake up with it, then I know the truth!!!

Day 321 – *Feeling of the Day*: Reaching out for specialist help

No headache. Ergo, it's not the clock. Dang it, that would have been so easy to control! Regardless, no headache is good!!

On the flip side, not much bathroom success. I wonder if hair loss counts as a type of elimination. It's just the wrong one!

Major hair loss continues. I have a scary picture of the amount of hair I lost after one shower. Will not post that one!

I called my primary doctor to see if she could refer me to a dermatologist. Maybe it's the scalp and the hair issue is collateral damage, I wonder. She referred me to a hormone specialist instead. Thinking beyond my limited knowledge!

Day 322 – *Feeling of the Day*: Naughty

Mucho coffee time since my Mom arrived a week ago. I've been enjoying the afternoon coffees with fruit and sweets and leisurely talk, including mildly dramatic romance movies at night that I taped from the German TV. Mom REALLY likes those!

Only, after that movie Mom goes to bed and I watch one of my American TV shows, munching on chips or chocolate, around midnight. Not a good routine.

I will stop this tonight! I will watch only the news and maybe just the intro to the next episode with only one chip?

Day 323 – *Feeling of the Day*: Focusing on the good stuff

It's my birthday party today!! My real birthday is not until next Thursday, but Rob will be traveling that whole week including the weekend, so we had to move it up a bit. A smorgasbord of food selections will be served since the party is potluck style.

The only thing I know of that's on its way here is the fabulous mixed berry pie from the vegan bakery, curtesy of Tanya who's on her way to our house as we speak (as I write...). I'm good with that!! Keeping my eyes on the pie. Focused!

Day 324 – *Feeling of the Day*: Full!

Umfph, I'm still full!

I managed to save one small sliver of the birthday pie for today, but everything else went yesterday. So good! Everybody liked the vegan mixed berry pie; nobody complained about a no-food issue! ☺

Also, I have an appointment with a hormone specialist on Tuesday, so that he can check my thyroid, etc. to see if this may be the cause for my hair loss. Can't wait...!

Day 326 – *Feeling of the Day*: Definitely not satisfied

Well, Doc Hormone confirmed it's not a hormone issue. He told me to wait and see if things will get better. Hair loss can be caused by so many different things ("Really!!!"). If things don't improve by October, my next step would be to see a (wait for it) dermatologist!!

Wow! Didn't see that one coming!

Day 327 – *Feeling of the Day*: **Excited with new food discovery, again**

Thai food – Sweet and sour (clear) sauce with steamed tofu and stuff (aka veggies) is YUMMY!!!

This works! ☺ (Can you tell, I'm still excited every time I find new food to eat!)

My mom is still visiting. I think, she's secretly looking at my food, especially my kale, veggie or quinoa burgers and thinking, "Wow, what's happening here?!?!?!?? Why is my daughter eating what looks like a bunch of medallions??"

Day 328 – *Feeling of the Day*: I'm the birthday girl!

My birthday!!! "It's my party and I'll eat if I want to, eat if I want to, EAT if I want to!" Oh, yeah!

Well, I did, but nothing dangerous or forbidden. Most of my day today was spent at the furniture store, picking lead-free dishes (FINALLY!!!) and a new sleeper couch for our guest room. This resulted in a piece of salmon, French fries and a cup of Swedish coffee for lunch.

We ate out (again) for dinner. This time with my boys. I had a roasted veggie salad in which I only substituted the artichokes (not my thing) for garbanzo beans, switched the dressing to oil and vinegar (which according to the blood type diet, I shouldn't consume). I think I'm getting really good at this substitution thing!

The crowning moment was a sorbet and soy cappuccino for dessert. Man, I can't believe that that is considered an indulgence for me now. Things used to be so different.

Aahhh, the good ole' days!

On another note, I've also finally picked glass containers to replace all my plastic food containers. I could not find square or rectangular glass containers with glass lids. They all still have plastic lids, but I figure, that's still better than all plastic. And no container materials state "BPA-free and BSA-free". No such thing! So, I went ahead and bought some containers online with BPA-free plastic lids. Better than stressing over this any longer! I'm making progress!!

My credit card is about to explode!!

Day 329 – *Feeling of the Day*: Seeing the light at the end of a long tunnel

I can't believe it's September, and I am entering month number 11 on my one-year journey! Technically, the sixth of September is the mark of the monthiversary, but I'm feeling generous today when counting days.

I can't believe time is coming close!!!

But with my luck, Doc is going to see me on my next appointment and say, "Not one year. I meant TWO years!!!"

Better not jinx it! Ok, I take it back!!

Day 331 – *Feeling of the Day*: Organized

I don't even remember what I've been eating these days. I've been too busy losing hair!

Actually, some kind of remodel-and-upgrade bug got a hold of me and besides replacing all my plastic food containers with glass and replacing our dishes, I went through my kitchen cabinets and drawers and reorganized the whole thing to fit all the new and take out EVERYTHING I don't use!!

Boys are running around the place, scratching their heads and going, "We used to have bowls? Where are they? What happened to the little plates??"

Reorganizing is one of my favorite things, which is why I help other people declutter their homes and lives now for $$. I used to work in the corporate world, but this is so much more fun! So, reorganizing my own home is great! And doing it with my Mom is that much more fun!! Therefore, I'm taking this opportunity to take Mom all over the place, playing house! ☺

Day 332 – *Feeling of the Day*: Rushed

Today, we prepped the guest room for painting, painted, did all the touch-ups, put the new couch together and placed it into the guest room (which is Mom's room for now), took out all the furniture that doesn't belong there anymore, and finally shifted some other furniture in the house to update the look of the living room as well.

Then sushi lunch!

After that, moving on to buying school supplies; those last bits that are on the latest list of demands, but mostly all sold out. I don't get it. Why do some teachers/schools recommend you wait until school starts before buying all the supplies? The teachers will tell the students what they'd like specifically; but by that time, the stores are nearly sold out! Who came up with that system?!? "Stores, listen up! Keep some supplies for the time when school starts!! Please!!!"

I found ONE three-subject spiral notebook today in the entire office supply store. ONE!!

And I fought for it, too!!

Then, grocery shopping. Then, dinner. Then, putting all the dates for the school year into my calendar. Then, answering some teacher texts, downloading the new teacher-requested apps, kiss the boys good night, then, spending some time with Mom before nearly falling asleep on the couch! Man, it's almost midnight!

I must set my alarm to 6am for a swim test at Aaron's school as pre-requisite for his surf team participation. Yeah, good idea! Should know how to swim if one wants to surf.

Now finally going to bed. I didn't even read this month's book club book! ☹

Maybe better luck next month or in my next life?!?

Day 333 – *Feeling of the Day:* Not fine

I do not like the fact that headaches have crept back into my life! ☹ It's been very hot, but that didn't seem to be an issue just a few months ago.

Ever since all the traveling (mostly after Korea), I've been having light headaches again. A couple of weeks ago, it's been several times per week. Just enough to not enjoy tilting my head, but not so bad that I'd take medicine. This is not good!

I'm not sure what to make of it, maybe making all the hairs fall out of my head is some kind of stress on the brain?!?

Today was another day with a super busy schedule and it's a hot day, too. This should not have been a headache factor anymore, but here it is.

I'm going to sleep! Grumpy!! ☹

Day 334 – *Feeling of the Day*: As if I can taste the Grand Finale

Today marks a very special day! It's my 11-months monthsiversary of the 'No Food' diet! I can't believe I reached this milestone, I'm almost there!!

Unfortunately, by next month, I don't think Doc will let me off the gluten/dairy/chicken/yeast/nuts and seeds hook. I have a feeling that the inflammation in my gut is not 100% healed (checking my tongue, it's not quite all rounded yet with an even edge like it should be). Also, lingering headaches, which may be caused by stress, but you never know. And then the hair loss, which continues, apparently, until I am completely bald?!?

So, I don't think I'll be able to go back to my old self, and actually, I wouldn't want to. Didn't I get rid of the pain in my joints, the bloated feelings, most migraines, cleared my skin (mostly) and also feel trimmer? I sure did!

But in any case, here's to 11 months and just one more to go on my official journey! I really, really cannot believe it!

I just had an idea of how I could perhaps celebrate this upcoming one-year-anniversary. Maybe, just maybe! I'll have to prepare this a little, and I'm not sure if I can set it all up without help but let's see. I might make this work. It'll be fun and truly for fun only!

Not ready to divulge any details, in case it doesn't work out.

Day 336 – *Feeling of the Day*: Looking forward to my next visit with Doc

Yessssss, Doc has returned to the motherland and I'll be seeing him on September 18th. Funny how I am looking forward to seeing him for another chelation IV to see if anything's changed. My idea of 'fun' sure has changed!

I've been surviving being out and about organizing the new school year, more work, and Mom's visit by picking through menu choices and omitting the offenders, just as I have for most of this past year. I think this might be one of the biggest takeaways from the whole experience (besides improving my health), which is how to eat out without allowing all of the allergens into my tummy. I guess, that's a skill, too.

And I might need it after I see Doc!

Doc will say that it's okay to ease up on the restrictions but take it very slowly. It would probably never be back to eating whatever I want whenever I want to;

OR

He'll say that I'm not ready to go back to adding those foods and will just have to stay away from them for good.

Either way, I think I'm screwed! But those are the two options I can potentially see coming my way.

Way to go, Ms. Optimistic!! ☹

Day 338 – *Feeling of the Day*: Looking at the bright side

Headache again!! Man!!!!!!

But here's something refreshing. I just read that it's a good idea to give your skin a rest from all the enhancing products and use nothing but eye cream and moisturizer for a time period of about 40 days.

I'm totally up for that because it means I have less sh#t to do! ☺

I will be done with this experiment on October 20th! Not sure, however, how I will be spending the extra time that I'll gain until then. I do have a few ideas.

Day 339 – *Feeling of the Day*: Trying too hard

First fail in restaurant meal substitution strategy! I was trying to order fish tacos today, but the menu stated that the fish was in a panko crust. I asked if I could have the fish grilled instead.

The waiter said, "No, but they could pan fry the fish."

I said, "That'll work, but in oil, please (if anything at all), no butter."

Waiter said, "Okay."

Then I asked about the tacos, turns out they were half flour, half corn (I don't dare thinking about whether I had those before!)

I said no to that. Now I have fish tacos with pan-fried fish instead of crusty fish and without tacos.

Then I said, "Please leave out the sauce, too (creamy chipotle sauce)."

The waiter asked what I wanted with the fish if no tacos, no sauce, and no chips on the side?

I thought about it for a moment and said, "I guess I'll have the grilled veggie salad after all."

Day 340 – *Feeling of the Day*: Pondering

My birthday came and went, and I totally forgot about making it my Big Day of Wheat!!! I FORGOT!!!

Now, here's a question for the philosophers: If you lost something (e.g. gluten in your food) and after awhile, you're allowed to have it again but maybe now it doesn't taste good anymore because you got used to not having it, did you really lose something?!??

I don't want to imply that I no longer crave gluten or dairy. I sometimes really, really do. Coffee time has never been the same because I mainly rotate the three to four types of cookies that I can have. Same goes for the milk (rotating coconut and soy creamer and vanilla pea milk). But if I was allowed to have real milk again, what if I didn't like the taste now?

I can't help but wonder.

Day 341 – *Feeling of the Day*: Bummed out

I had a lovely book club meeting last night with lovely ladies (as usual), and in spite of the fact that the library ate my copy of the book and I had been unable to read most of it, the evening progressed with a lively discussion.

We not only discuss; we also eat together as each meeting is a potluck affair. The very lovely hostess Meghan had made roasted root vegetables, which I winked at (the veggies, not the hostess), and baked chicken on a separate dish. I was delighted! Roasted veggies have become one of my favorites, and it was a pleasant and gluten-free surprise! I piled as much as I could onto my plate and complemented said veggies with a rice and edamame-mix as well as green salad.

As we are sitting and enjoying the dinner, everybody compliments the food, swishing their wine in their glasses and the setting is so classy, I can't help but feel a little out of place. I don't drink because I never took a liking to alcohol.

So, here I am stuffing my face with roast veggies when one of the ladies asked Meghan how she had prepared the dish. Meghan happily describes how she combines the vegetables with olive oil and various herbs, spreads them on a baking pan and then places the chicken on top while baking it. Therefore, the juice of the chicken drips through and onto the vegetables and that gives them the extra special flavor! Noooooooooooo!

My jaw stopped dead in its tracks! I am so bummed like I haven't been in a while over food. I can't eat the roast veggies now! ☹ And boy, did I dig in until that very moment!

I quietly got up, went to the counter with all the foods and filled my plate with some more rice/edamame mix. I was so sad. I really, really wanted to eat chocolate and pull the covers over my head.

Thankfully, the group is so fun and there was so much distraction once we started our discussion that, very quickly, everything turned into a great night.

At the very end, I dared myself to make a little announcement concerning my plan on how to commemorate the one-year anniversary of my no-food diet. I'm so excited, and everybody cheered me on. I hope, I really hope, I can make it work!

Day 342 – *Feeling of the Day*: Disconcerted

Hubby bought a large pack of toilet paper online without the toilet paper roll inside. I mean, there's no cardboard roll on the very inside of it. Cutting back on cardboard usage is probably a good idea, but I can't wait to reach the end of the first roll to see what happens when I'm down to just about three sheets. Will it slide down and fall on the ground until I am ready to use those last three sheets? Or is there some magic to this 'no roll' roll?

One can only wait and see.

Day 343 – *Feeling of the Day*: Brave, to a certain extent

I've been meaning to cut back on the supplement capsules that I take daily, so I switched from the fish oil capsule to the real thing, actual fish oil. I was very brave when I bought it, and I took a tablespoon full this morning before breakfast. Bwuaaaaaaaaaaaaaah!!

I don't think I need to eat for the rest of the day! ☹

Day 344 – *Feeling of the Day*: In the danger zone

Yup, the last three sheets of toilet paper just slide down and fall on the ground. That's where they reside now until I put on a new roll and balance them over the new roll.

The real danger in this 'no roll' toilet paper roll is that once the last roll is finished that I keep in the bathroom drawer, I have no cardboard roll to take to the kitchen in order to remind me to take new rolls out of the garage and put them back into the bathroom drawer for refills.

This could get ugly!

Day 345 – *Feeling of the Day*: All bad

What a miserable day today! I woke up at 5am with a headache. I had a glass of water and tried to go back to sleep and I did, but no good quality sleep. The pain never went away even after I I took half a pain pill.

My fingers were also hurting again just slightly in the mornings. I might need to lay off the party animal lifestyle, having after-dinner espresso and something to snack on later in the evening while watching TV with Mom.

Also, major hair loss again in the shower, shocking! I'm surprised there's anything left.

Then we took my Mom to the airport early in the afternoon for her flight back to Germany. That was sad because I really love my Mom and we had a good time doing lots of stuff around the house and fun times with the boys as well.

Now we're supposed to go to Germany in the winter for my Dad's 80th birthday and Christmas, but the airline we booked our flights with just filed bankruptcy. We'll have to wait and see if other airlines will take over the planes and routes AND honor the tickets that have been sold for flights in December/January. ☹

I even felt like throwing up in the car on the way to the airport this afternoon. I'm not feeling good at all today.

Day 346 – *Feeling of the Day*: Taking stock

Doc visit today! New restrictions. It had been so long (over four months) that I saw Doc, we had lots to talk about on our travels, politics, music, etc.

We also talked about my health, the state of my diet, the hair (Doc has no idea either) and my question if a person should take iodine as a supplement? Doc says if I get seaweed and other sea vegetables in my diet, it should be enough.

As to the recent health issues (mostly due to irregular and unsupervised ingredients while eating out; lots and lots of it while traveling), Doc suggested that I go gluten-free for three months more, counting from the time I got back from Korea. That was August 6th, so my new deadline for the Big Day of Wheat is November 6th.

Not too bad, especially since October 6th was my original one-year mark. As I mentioned before, I was planning on going until the end of October anyway because of last year's Christmas cheating, etc.

Although we ate out a lot while Mom was here, I am pretty sure that I didn't commit any gluten infractions. Pretty sure? I think?

Then, I got another IV to take on the heavy metals again. Twinkle came and did her sparkly magic, pinning down the one vein that'll allow her to pop in the IV needle and pump me full of whatever chelation agent.

After an hour and a half when I was done, I suddenly felt as if I had a something stuck in my throat. It was the weirdest thing and lasted until after dinner! Regardless of me drinking some water and even eating something, the strange 'blockage' was there. I could still swallow, but it was definitely more than weird.

Well, this day also had the elegant touch of peeing in the bucket over a six-hour time span (so I can send a mixed specimen to the lab and have them tell me how bad things are), and having to drink my non-lovely orange powder drink. Three more tomorrow! Oh boy! I'm just now finishing today's last 'deposit'.

Tired! I'll go to bed because I must wake Aaron tomorrow in time for the first surf meet. He must get up at 5:30am. Me, too.

Day 347 – *Feeling of the Day*: Stupid!

Seriously, how dumb can I be?!?!?!!

How bad of a cook can I possibly be???

Mom had brought some sauce mixes from Germany that I use to make Bolognese sauce for pasta. Everybody in the family loves this sauce and the sauce mix is a new kind, free of gluten, yeast and other No-Nos. I fixed the meat and poured the first bag of sauce mix into the pan, then added the water and decided that I had so much meat that I should add a second little baggie and more water. I opened a second bag, poured it on and screamed because this powder was yellow curry instead of Bolognese mix!

I didn't look at the front of the bag, even though I knew Mom had brought a variety of baggies!

How stupid!!!

I quickly grabbed a spoon and tried to eliminate as much curry from my Bolognese as possible. But of course, it was impossible to get everything out clean.

So, Bolognese with a slight hint of curry for tonight's dinner!

Day 348 – *Feeling of the Day*: In pain again

Another day with a bad headache, which started early in the morning. This one was bad enough for me to surrender to a whole pain pill right away and go to bed after I took Lucas to school. I slept until 2pm and it was better. Drank lots of water.

Doc had classified my recent headaches as tension headaches, and I whole-heartedly agreed. I have not done any formal exercise over the summer (with the exception of shopping marathons with Mom and some snorkeling without Mom but with fishies in Hawaii); no yoga or stretching of any kind, only occasional walks. I just have not taken care of myself and now my body is quickly reacting to such mistreatment!

I immediately started stretching. I will see Doc Chiropractor tomorrow and start exercising again!

Day 349 – *Feeling of the Day*: Hopeful

Man, what a busy day!! After the chiropractor, I had another appointment with someone helping me with my marketing works for my business and then finally got around to thinking about how to set up things for my one-year celebration on October 6th (for the no-food anniversary, of course).

It's the first day I am feeling I might get a handle on things and life might just slow down a tad after I got these things on their way. ☺

Day 350 – *Feeling of the Day*: Getting excited

After a work appointment in the afternoon, I saw my friend, Dena for dinner. I picked out curried cauliflower salad and some corn chips from the health food store and took that over to the coffee shop. That's how we roll!

We hadn't seen each other in a few months due to summer break, etc. We don't live close to each other either but meet at the monthly chapter meeting for professional organizers that we both attend.

I told her about my upcoming celebration, and she was very excited for me. Yay! ☺ She gave me some ideas on what I could include, to make it even more fun.

I can't wait!

Day 351 – *Feeling of the Day*: Like a couch potato

Things are not moving in my body – again! No surprise! I haven't been moving my body much either, despite very good intentions! Yesterday, for example, I saw Victoria for coffee in the morning (our first coffee since before summer break!!), and with all my determination, I hoped to go to yoga before driving down to my work appointment. Yoga didn't work out because hubby came home early, and we went to lunch. Then work, and then dinner with Dena (see above).

Today, I had even better intentions – get the kids off to school, go walk and then have a date with hubby (who is home today). I had to skip the walk because hubby was in a hurry to get out of the house and start the day.

Tomorrow??

Day 353 – *Feeling of the Day*: Coming to terms with my hair

Yoga today, finally! I also planned on going into the sauna so that I could clean out my body through the skin, but the sauna and the whole pool area is closed for renovation this month. Too lazy to drive to another gym so I went home.

But still – Yoga! I did it!! ☺ Gotta celebrate those small successes!

For lunch, I prepared my cool kale burger with a side of hash browns, so my plate looked like I had a bunch of medallions on it. Hey, this one looks like a bronze, and this one more like a coal. Well, I must remember to not start something else while I am frying medallions in the pan!

Health update! The hair loss is starting to slow down, mainly because there isn't much left. I will go see my hairdresser to see if she can do some magic. I would really like a lion's mane style hairdo, but we'll see what she can do with my leftovers. Maybe a Farah Fawcett? Maybe only Yul Brunner?

Day 354 – *Feeling of the Day*: So full of anticipation

I cannot believe my one-year anniversary is only TEN days away!!! It seems so sudden! I really must make that day special and eat. Hmmm? What am I gonna eat?!?? Maybe just one liiiiiiitle piece of milk chocolate?!?!?!?? Maybe one bite of a crunchy baguette with Nutella?? Maybe a piece of pasta?!??

Maybe none of the above and all clean food but do something else fun? Oh yeah, right. Doc had said to go gluten-free through November 6, so not so much the baguette or pasta, but the milk chocolate. Or a lick of vanilla and caramel ice cream? A spoonful of Nutella without baguette? Works for me, too!!

Oh, the things I will eat; the places I'll go!!

Day 355 – *Feeling of the Day*: Disgusted

This has GOT to be one of the least successful coffee times of my life! I thought the pea milk tasted somewhat different this morning in my cornflakes, but in my coffee?!?!?!!!

Imagine ground up peas (with vanilla flavor) in your coffee, only the peas are on their way of going bad!

Not a pretty picture, I know! I tasted it!!

Day 356 – *Feeling of the Day*: Absolutely baffled

Now I am FLOORED!! I am stunned beyond belief!!!! Doc sent the latest lab results from last week's anti-heavy metal IV, and the level of lead went UP! By a lot!!!

HOW IN THE WORLD?!?!?!?!??!!!!! How could this be???

The very first measurement had been 30 units (of whatever), with under 2 units being within normal levels! That itself was shocking! Then it went down along with all other heavy metals to 24 units at the end of the 12-week treatment that I finished in April.

Last week we did one IV and the lab results just came in: Lead is at 36 units!!! HOW????

I'm not eating it! Or drinking lead tea!

I am so lost!!! I am starting to wonder if it is even possible to get rid of it at all?!

Depressed, I am going to lunch with Kate. ☹☹

Day 357 – *Feeling of the Day*: Ugh

Doc confirmed my appointment for this coming Monday and for the time being, all the Mondays thereafter. I guess there'll be lots of Monday-Twinkle around. ☹

Déjà-vu!!!!!

Day 358 – *Feeling of the Day*: Disheartened

Man, I gotta say, I'm so discouraged! I thought this year was going to go so well and overall, things would improve. Instead, my heavy metals are worse, the hair is still falling out, no sign of slowing down and I have a cold!

I really got used to lots of things over this past year, and I am not missing my daily chocolate dose anymore, but still! Give me a break!!

Fine, I'll suck it up and go with more flow, again. ☹

Only six (6!!!) more days until my one-year anniversary, and then one more month of gluten-free and everything else-free (I think). This is indeed hard to believe!

Day 359 – *Feeling of the Day*: Questioning all things

It is here! The first day of October, which means it is my anniversary month!!!!! Unbelievably, I've made it, but it has been long! I must admit it!

I think my attitude has also slowly but surely changed. I always remember when Doc first told me what I had to change and after a loooooooooong discussion over what exactly remained as food for me, he finally said: "And, if you occasionally ever feel like you want just one little bite of something, then it's okay. Go ahead and have a bite."

It was very clear from that discussion that this was meant for the very occasional urge only. But recently, I've used that statement more often than I should have. I guess feeling that I'm almost at the one-year mark, I figured I can slowly have another bite of one or the other forbidden foods.

For example, during lunch with Kate the other day, I ordered, "Fish tacos, not breaded, no cheese or other dairy, please!" I thought I had remembered all the stipulations. However, when I ate the fish, I realized that there was some kind of sauce on the bottom of the taco that tasted like mayonnaise, which contains egg. I ate the whole thing anyway. BAD, BAD, Annette!!! ☹

I should probably wait for Doc's 'Go ahead', but I am so tired of the restrictions and discouraged (see above) about the lab results, that I'm starting to question the whole undertaking.

I know this is not a good attitude. I need to pick myself up. Hmm, well, I will go see Doc tomorrow (and be cheered on by Twinkle), so maybe some talk about the whole situation will help me get back on track.

Plus, I've done plenty of 'one-year-experiences' in my life, so I know I can do such a thing. I've lived in Paris, Tokyo, Los Angeles and on Maui each for a year. I know how to tackle a timed experiment of this length!

I just hope Doc won't extend the whole thing by much more than this one month into November. Ok, positive thoughts now! ☺

Day 361 – *Feeling of the Day*: Got some resolution, small relief

Mixed news out of Doc's office!

First, he called the lab about my last test results. Both he and the lab person agreed that something must have been off when taking the sample. It's possible that the levels of certain metals may go up again, but certainly not by 50% over the course of six months!

This calls for a redo of the lab work, which is scheduled for next Monday. Now, if I could only remember each day not to eat fish (because of heavy metals in fish!). They WILL alter the results, so no fish for 10 days before the test, per Doc.

Secondly, Doc is thinking of retiring.

I said, "Not before my lead is gone!!"

That news actually came as a shocker. I'd never thought I'd have to find someone else pulling precious metals out of me! Hmmm. Besides, that new person, whoever, better be using Twinkle to stick me with that needle! She is magical! ☺

Day 362 – *Feeling of the Day*: Aged

I don't know if this 40-day experiment with no face care products (except for eye cream and moisturizer) is working for me. I feel as if I've aged by about 5 years – maybe 10.

Even Doc said the other day to me, "You look different! Something? Are you alright?"

I said, "Well, I have this cold and I've been really busy and so, I'm tired."

He says, "No, I'm not sure. Maybe the eyes? Something's just different."

Now, we all know that "different" is code for "terrible"! So, I guess, this may not work for me.

I'll be going back to adding toner and serum, just as soon as I have the time again. It's too bad because I had already planned on using all this extra time that I am saving to sort through my pictures on the phone and possibly clean out my garage.

So, that won't get done AGAIN!

Day 364 – *Feeling of the Day*: Getting ready to celebrate

Gee, I'm having a hard time! Who knew that setting up this special thing to celebrate TOMORROW'S one-year anniversary of no food would be so hard?!?!?!!! It's something people do all the time! I've been planning and organizing for at least several days now.

Anyways, I cannot even believe, tomorrow is the day! ☺

Aaaand, I just noticed that I haven't had those tension headaches during the last two weeks. Maybe, things will be alright after all. I'll end up super healthy, be eating well and become super fit (once I add strength exercises). And I'll live perfectly ever after! But with my luck, then I'll probably get hit by the bus!

OK, back to work!

Day 365 – *Feeling of the Day*: Jubilant!!

IT'S HERE!!! TODAY IS THE DAY! I MADE IT THROUGH ONE YEAR!

This is how I am going to celebrate: I AM WRITING A BOOK!!!!!

Yup, same one you're reading right now, I've come this far!

First, I started with a blog. Let me tell you that I had a heck of a time setting it up! Self-hosted website management systems are NOT your friend when you're somewhat uninterested in the technical aspects of setting up a website. With a little bit of help from a new friend (who knows tech!!) and the friendly tech support at the webhosting service, I've been able to set it up. And now I have a book! I am excited!

Also: Celebration number 2: I went a had a facial! ☺

Celebration number 3: I will have a spoonful of Nutella or maybe a piece of cheese? Still undecided. I can't believe I haven't had an egg or nuts in over a year now.

Celebration number 4: Will go out to dinner with the boys (hubby out of town).

Tomorrow, I will recuperate and finally think about what all changed for me during this year and write my findings to share with Doc.

Later that night:

Celebration number 3 turned out to be the spoonful of Nutella – the tiny kind of spoon. OMG! It was so good!! ☺

It's the good Nutella, hand-carried from Germany (Mom brought it when she came to visit last month), and this one still tastes better to me than the American version (this is me being a Nutella snob!). I just smelled it at first and that was almost good enough, but not quite. I dipped the little espresso spoon into the glass jar, piled little Mount Everest onto the spoon and just took a little bit of it at first.

Aaaaaahhh, that just melted on my tongue!

The rest of the spoonful was gone in one quick moment, but I was careful not to eat the spoon itself! Oh boy, that was one of the best things all day!

"Nutella, you complete me!" ☺

Day 366 – *Feeling of the Day*: Amused

I talked to hubby about how to write my book because I was wondering if I should include people's real names (first names only!) or if I should change the names.

He thought about it for a moment and said, "I think I would like to be called 'Sebastian'. Or maybe 'Alejandro'! Or maybe 'Sebastian-Alejandro'! What do you think??"

I looked at him, him being a full-blooded Korean, blinked a few times and said, "You know, you don't look like an 'Alejandro' at all!" That did not even faze him; he kept on going, trying out what it would sound like if he were Sebastian-Alejandro.

"Yeah, 'Sebastian-Alejandro'! Hey, my name is Sebastian-Alejandro! Hi, I'm Sebastian-Alejandro!"

Then he asked me, "How do you spell 'Sebastian'? Or 'Alejandro'?"

I said, "If you can't spell it, you can't have it! Besides, I'm gonna write about this in my book!"

He answered, "I'm not talking to you!"

That lasted about 45 seconds. I shall call him 'Rob' in my book. ☺

Day 367 – *Feeling of the Day*: Like summarizing the last 12 months

Sooooooo, I've been thinking about this whole experience and am going to try to recap the big stuff. Here I go!

What changed for me during this past year:

1. The joint pain in my fingers: Gone
2. Migraines: Gone (this is huge!!!)
3. Periodic gum inflammations: Gone
4. Bloated feeling (mostly after eating out): Gone
5. Lost 7 pounds (mostly from lack of milk chocolate)
6. Lost hair (apparently not related to either diet or hormones)
7. I am left with 163 packs of soy sauce (don't let hubby find out about this!)
8. I learned how to substitute ingredients really well, even at the restaurant, so that the meal will fit my specific needs
9. I know I can travel and still largely adhere to my diet
10. More constipation recently, but handling it with prune juice or plums
11. I'm eating lots more variety, sometimes scary foods
12. I learned that rotating foods is the best way to minimize possible overload in my system

Things that didn't change:

1. I am still not a good cook (but I continue to try)
2. I definitely still don't know how to make broccoli tasty
3. My kids still complain about new foods (and there are a lot more of those now than in my prior gluten and dairy-full life), but I guess, this will be a challenge until they grow up or move out, whichever comes first

Other things that I learned or practice now:

1. Being on a restricted diet automatically eliminates all the random snacking when offered to taste new items at the market, therefore it cuts down on surprise calories.

2. The easiest places for eating out when following a gluten-free and dairy-free diet are:
    a. Asian restaurants (except watch the teriyaki and soy sauce!)
    b. Mexican foods (hold the cheese and butter!)
    c. Salads (might need to modify the dressing to simple oil and vinegar and possibly substitute other Ingredients; hold the cheese and croutons)
3. Many, many Italian restaurants in my area are now carrying gluten-free pizza crusts and some even offer gluten-free pasta, you just have to ask.
4. No more raw foods after 4pm (if possible), therefore salads rather for lunch than dinner.
5. Last meal of the day about four to six hours before bedtime. This is not always realistic, but I keep trying. This rule cuts down on the snacking in front of the TV at night big time!
6. The safest and healthiest way to eat is to prepare meals at home instead of eating out. This allows for complete control over the ingredients and in fact, with some substitution as needed, I can eat almost anything I want.

Life is getting a lot easier even with these restrictions!

Day 385 – *Feeling of the Day*: Very, very relieved

I think I am coming to a very positive end soon! I saw Doc today for another IV. Lab results are in for the second test, the redo, after the previous catastrophic results (lead at 36 units). Indeed, something must have gone wrong during that first test, because the latest results show that almost all heavy metals are now in check, either in the green or just slightly in the yellow area, except for lead that is still in the red.

But it is DOWN to 17 units!! The bar on the chart is actually not touching the edge of the paper anymore!! In other words, the result is no longer off the chart, and since I am continuing with my chelation for this second round, I am positive that it will continue to go down!

BIG YAY!!!!! ☺

After all this good news, I had to go by the local gluten-free bakery and buy my favorite personal pie in order to celebrate, the mixed berry pie. So yummy! The last time I bought it, Rob/Sebastian-Alejandro ate almost half of it!

Also, I went to see the dermatologist regarding my hair, and she finally gave me clarity. The first round of chelation sent my body into somewhat of a shock mode and my hair follicles responded by going dormant earlier than normal.

She explained that hair follicles have a normal cycle of three phases: Growth, being dormant, and falling out. So, in simplified terms, about one third of the hair all over the head will be in one of those stages. In my case, more hair follicles had gone dormant than normal and when the 'falling out period' started, a lot more hair came out than the usual amount.

In any case, she strongly reassured me that I wasn't going to be bald, and she prescribed medicine, which I now have to apply to the scalp twice a day, in order to strengthen and encourage stronger regrowth. Voilà! I'll have more fuzz to fall out after the current chelation therapy! ;)

The only bummer is that part of that regrowth is coming in gray and somewhat frizzy. My normal hair is blonde and very fine, but I guess, with some gray frizzy action in my hair, I will finally have the one thing I've dreamed of my entire life – VOLUME!!

Day 389 – *Feeling of the Day*: Curious

Doc has found a replacement doc who will take over his practice. I shall meet him in about two weeks during one of the IV sessions. I still want to do my Big Day of Wheat sometime soon, because there's only ONE SINGLE WEEK left to go before it's time for that chelation series!

I hope Doc stays around long enough so that we can discuss the results of that!

Soon, so soon! I can almost taste it!

Day 399 – *Feeling of the Day*: Thrilled

This is it! It is FINALLY here, it's happening!!! Today is my "Big Day of Wheat" Eve! I am so excited!

When I went to see Doc again last Monday, he smiled and gave me the green light to go ahead and start reintroducing food choices that I've not had anywhere between nine to thirteen months! He asked me what I wanted to try out first, and since wheat had been on my radar all this time, it seemed like the natural choice.

Nevertheless, it occurred to me that milk would be equally good: Cheese! Yogurt! Ice cream! MILK CHOCOLATE! If wheat goes well, milk will be my next choice ;)

And then Nutella (hazelnuts!)

And then yeast, so that I can eat random baked goods.

And at some point, eggs! Doc told me that some people, who have omitted eggs for this long, have a really hard time (they throw up when they first eat egg again). I'll see. One step at a time!

Doc told me to take very detailed notes of everything that's going on with my body for a couple of days before my Big Day of Wheat, the day of, and another two days after to see if I have any kind of reaction. I've been documenting my food, drink, bathroom experiences and anything else I could think of for two days now. And since I've been planning this day for the last nine months, I already know what I'm going to have tomorrow.

I went to the supermarket with Lucas and picked out all the food items for tomorrow. This consisted of bran flakes for breakfast, fusilli pasta for lunch, my favorite mint cookies for coffee time and finally a sourdough bread (without yeast!) for dinner. I am so excited, it's like Christmas!

I might not even be able to sleep! ☺

Day 400 – *Feeling of the Day*: Ecstatic and watchful at the same time

MY BIG DAY OF WHEAT!!!!

It's like my birthday and Christmas combined! I am so excited!

I did indeed sleep very badly (last night's espresso?!?), but I am up and nervous, but happy. I feel as if I have a first date with wheat! ☺

First up: Breakfast! I had bran flakes mixed with oats and dried fruit with pea milk. When I lifted that first spoonful of bran flakes both Aaron and Lucas watched me intently waiting for my head to explode or something. We all laughed; I took the spoonful. BOY! Did that taste good!

Lucas said, "It's good, huh?!? See, this tastes so much better" as he is munching on his cinnamon squares. Not what I want to portray. I want them to know that it's healthier to eat all kinds of different foods and so of course, I had to say, "Well, the other cereal tastes good, too! But this is a taste I haven't had for a year!"

It really did taste so yummy! I'm sad that breakfast is over, but Lucas then comforted me by saying, "I bet you are looking forward to lunch! I know I am!"

I am, too. So far, feeling good, full of energy and waiting to tackle my exciting day of laundry, dishes, taking the kids around, and some work on the computer. Wow!

10am: Still feeling fine. This is weird, but good.

1pm: Lunch! Pasta Bolognese (sauce homemade with the help of a sauce mix) and grilled veggies, yuuuuummmy! I felt full afterwards, but then I had a big plate full. I need to take advantage of today's special!!

4pm: Still all good. Nothing weird popping up. All good!

5pm: Coffee time. I'm having my fruit and I bought cookies that I used to LOVE! They are the sandwich-type with a mint cream filling. But right as I finished the fruit, Aaron called and asked if I could pick him up from the skate park with his friend. Coffee interrupted!

7pm: Sourdough bread (no yeast!) for dinner, dipped in olive oil and balsamic vinegar. ☺ Hey, it qualifies as dinner in my world!

Also, I finished the coffee because I am eating those cookies that I bought just for this grand occasion!

Sadly, neither the bread nor the cookies tasted as good as I remembered. I am really surprised especially about the cookies! I used to buy these as a treat, and now this?!?

It makes me wonder. Why would I even want to bring wheat back into my diet, knowing that it's not a good idea to eat that much of it anyhow? Especially if it's not as tasty as I thought!! I might have to rethink my future.

I would be happy if I could ease up on the extremely strict diet, but truly, I don't think I would want to go back to all those foods that aren't doing me any good and don't add exceptional excitement to my plate!

Day 401 – *Feeling of the Day*: Still observant

No obvious reaction to anything. Still taking detailed notes, but nothing has jumped out at me. This might be good after all! ☺

Day 402 – *Feeling of the Day*: I'm fine!

Still no adverse reaction to my Big Day of Wheat. I think I can see Doc tomorrow and report back with good news. ☺

Day 403 – *Feeling of the Day*: Cautiously very optimistic

I talked with Doc about my wheat experience. He suggested that I do the experiment one more time, just for good measure and to be sure. Maybe my allergies were sleeping that day? All in all, he was happy to hear that things have improved, but gave me a note of caution: Do not go out and date wheat again! In fact, he thinks it's just not a good idea to be thinking about wheat much at all (or eat it.)

Next up is my repeat experiment and then start challenging all the other stuff such as dairy, eggs, etc. Slowly, but surely, find out what works and what doesn't.

Well, I'm pretty happy with what I've found out this year, all the new foods I actually enjoy instead of relying on wheat or dairy; I'm also happy about everything I learned, and I am really, really happy without migraines and all the other stuff!

In the end, I might just live. In fact, I might even live really well for that matter! ☺

"Conclusion"

Six months later. After the last round of chelation finished, my new replacement Doc (whom I like very much) had me take all the tests again, the allergy test as well as the heavy metal test.

I was so nervous about the results but couldn't wait for them either.

Finally, the day of judgment came.

My food allergies and sensitivities have all vastly improved! I can now go back to having all foods once in a while that still have one evil star (mainly in the dairy section), but overall such a BIG improvement!

I will cut out gluten for good, as long as I am in the US. In Europe, wheat seems to be less processed and therefore much more tolerable. I've heard this from several friends and Doc confirmed it, too.

I am super happy!!

The only food left with three evil red stars on the chart is Brazil nuts! Go figure! I haven't had those in at least a year and a half! Well, I can live without those nuts!

As for the heavy metals, even more of a surprise, EVERYTHING was in the green! A couple of metals were measuring borderline to the second level, not great, but also not terrible. So, it's all good, all around!

Doc will give me a mild powder drink that chelates the last bits of metals without the heavy impact on minerals in my body. I can do this on my own.

I am going to Germany in the summer and I WILL have my roll with Nutella and eat the whole darn thing!!! Not just one bite, oh no! I will eat the whole, top and bottom, and probably lick the Nutella off the knife, too! There, I said it! ☺

Well, I learned so much through this experience, practical as well as mental. Cutting out foods that don't go over well within my body is such a small sacrifice compared to the benefits!

And mostly, I learned that it is my own responsibility to take care of my health. Nobody else will tell me how to live well. I must take the first step of wanting to improve my health, and then I can go and seek help. But it's all possible.

The information as well as numerous products are widely available, online or in local stores, in the US as well as in Europe. That I know for sure and it makes a life with diet restrictions much easier than I initially thought possible. I just must be willing to experiment a bit and taste test a few things.

So, I tell myself: "You better appreciate every day and every moment and take charge!"

Live can be so good! ☺

Made in the USA
Monee, IL
17 February 2020